International Migration, U.S. Immigration Law and Civil Society:

From the Pre-Colonial Era to the 113th Congress

2014
Scalabrini International Migration Network
New York

The Scalabrini International Migration Network (SIMN) is a not-for-profit organization established by the Missionaries of Saint Charles, Scalabrinians, to safeguard the dignity and the rights of migrants, refugees, seafarers, itinerants and people on the move worldwide.

The opinions expressed in this book are solely those of the authors and do not necessarily reflect the opinions of the Scalabrini International Migration Network (SIMN).

International Migration, U.S. Immigration Law and Civil Society:

From the Pre-Colonial Era to the 113th Congress

First Edition

Copyright © 2014 by

Scalabrini International Migration Network Inc.

307 E 60th Street

New York 10022–1505

Tel. +1 (212) 913-0207 Email: advocacy@simn-cs.net

Published by: Scalabrini International Migration Network (SIMN).

Coordinator: Leonir Mario Chiarello, Executive Director of SIMN.

Editors: Leonir Mario Chiarello, Executive Director of SIMN and Donald Kerwin, Executive Director of the Center for Migration Studies of New York (CMS).

Proofreading: Breana George, Research Coordinator of CMS.

Layout: Josue Bustillo.

Cover design: Josue Bustillo and Diego Carámbula.

Historic photographs: Center for Migration Studies of New York.

Other photographs: http://www.shutterstock.com/

ISBN-978-0-9960560-0-7

Table of Contents

Preface

International Migration, U.S. Immigration Law and Civil Society: From the Pre-Colonial Era to the 113th Congress is the tenth in a series of studies published by the Scalabrini International Migration Network (SIMN) on migration in the Western Hemisphere. The Congregation of the Missionaries of Saint Charles, Scalabrinians, is an international community of Catholic priests and religious dedicated to serving migrants and refugees throughout the world. SIMN supports a network of more than 270 Scalabrinian migrant shelters, service centers, schools, research institutes and other programs along migrant corridors and in immigrant-receiving communities. Based on this work, it has direct knowledge on the need for effective, rights-respecting migration policies.

This volume follows a 2010 study on migration in the Western Hemisphere by Barry Mirkin, the former head of the population policy section of the United Nations (UN) Population Division, and subsequent studies on migration policy and civil society in Argentina, Brazil, Bolivia, Chile, Colombia, Mexico, Paraguay and Peru. The series seeks to improve migration governance in the Americas by educating policymakers and the public on the benefits, trade-offs and human dimensions of migration.

As with past volumes in this series, *International Migration, U.S. Immigration Law and Civil Society: From the Pre-Colonial Era to the 113th Congress* draws on the contributions of distinguished scholars and authors. Donald Kerwin, the Executive Director of the Center for Migration Studies of New York (CMS), introduces the volume. Joseph Chamie, the former director of the UN Population Division and past editor of the *International Migration Review*, provides an historic overview of migration flows and trends in the Americas, particularly in the United States. Charles Wheeler, a senior attorney at the Catholic Legal Immigration Network, Inc. (CLINIC) offers a succinct history of U.S. immigration law and policy, beginning with colonial era laws. Sara Campos, the former director of the Asylum Program for the Lawyers Committee for Civil Rights in San Francisco, documents the substantial role of civil society in immigration policymaking, advocacy, and service-provision.

The book illustrates the challenges in reaching policy consensus on these complex, contentious, and consequential issues. It highlights the central importance of immigration to the American experience and offers hope that the United States will reform its generous, but nonetheless outdated laws and broken immigration system.

Leonir Chiarello

Executive Director of SIMN

Introduction

Donald Kerwin

This book on U.S. immigration history, policy and civil society represents the tenth in a series produced by the Scalabrini International Migration Network (SIMN) on international migration to and within the Americas. Earlier volumes in the series have covered immigration policy and civil society in the Western Hemisphere and in eight countries: Argentina, Bolivia, Brazil, Chile, Colombia, Mexico, Paraguay and Peru. This volume provides a timely and accessible treatment of U.S. immigration flows, stocks, laws, policies and civil society. More than a primer, it identifies and analyzes the themes, trends and challenges that have driven U.S. immigration law and policy, leading to the current, unsettled debate on immigration reform.

The series draws on contributions from leading scholars and practitioners in the field. The U.S. immigration volume consists of chapters by Joseph Chamie, the former director of the United Nations Population Division, past director of research for the Center for Migration Studies of New York (CMS) and editor of the *International Migration Review*; Charles Wheeler, a senior attorney and director of training and legal support for the Catholic Legal Immigration Network, Inc. (CLINIC) and the former Executive Director of the National Immigration Law Center (NILC); and Sara Campos, a free-lance writer and the former director of the Asylum Program for the Lawyers Committee for Civil Rights in San Francisco.

Chamie begins the volume with a magisterial 525-year review of international migration to the Americas, English colonies in North America and the United States. He highlights the centrality of immigration to the growth of the Republic, as well as its costs and conflicts. Wheeler complements Chamie's analysis, with a history of U.S. immigration law and policy from colonial times to the present. He traces the forces that have shaped the U.S. immigration experience, including its "political movements—its diverse values, competing visions of nationality and membership, and... the human condition, with all its admirable and shameful qualities." Campos covers an issue that has received insufficient attention in the academic and popular literature: the growing influence of civil society on the U.S. immigration debate and in immigrant communities. Her account concentrates on the period between passage of the *Immigration Reform and Control Act of 1986* (IRCA) and the present.[1] This brief introduction will outline six themes that emerge from this volume.

Immigration Trends and Costs

Chamie stresses the scale and diversity of immigration to the United States, as well as its often fierce costs and trade-offs. An estimated fifty to 100 million people lived in the Americas prior to Christopher Columbus's landing, including as many as 10 million in the territory of the current United States. Migrant-born infectious diseases like smallpox, measles, chicken pox, malaria and yellow fever devastated native populations, killing (for example) ninety percent of those in the Massachusetts Bay area from 1618-1619. Between 1620 and 1865, nearly 600,000 slaves were brought to U.S. territory. More than one in seven perished at sea, and many more died in the course of their capture and transport to ship.

Perhaps more than one-half of immigrants to the colonies indentured themselves to wealthier colonialists, presaging similar arrangements throughout U.S. history. In the late nineteenth century, Chinese laborers ("coolies") worked to pay off the cost of their passage to the United States, often over the course of many years. Abusive labor conditions persist in many industries and occupations, particularly those with large numbers of unauthorized immigrants.

During the seventeenth and eighteenth centuries, as few as 400,000 persons immigrated to the United States. Yet colonial populations grew rapidly due to high birth rates (eight or more births per woman) and relatively low death rates. The nineteenth century brought rapid population increases due largely to immigration. Beginning in 1820, for seven consecutive decades, Ireland and Germany were the two top immigrant sending countries to the United States. Immigration from Italy, followed closely by Russia, spiked in the last decade of the nineteenth century and the first two decades of the twentieth century. Over the last five decades, Mexico has been the leading source of legal permanent residents (as well as unauthorized immigrants) to the United States, and has become the top migrant-sending country in U.S. history. Chamie could be referring to most immigrant groups in U.S. history when he writes that in the early 1900s Italian immigrants were depicted "as inferior, inept and prone

---

1 IRCA was the nation's last large-scale legalization legislation. It also created the employer sanctions programs and provided for increased border enforcement.

to crime because many lived in the worst areas of the towns where they settled and not infrequently experienced discrimination."

In the 1820s, fewer than 130,000 immigrants obtained legal permanent residence in the United States. This number leaped 2.8 million in the 1850s and to 8.2 million in the first decade of the twentieth century. The peak year for admission to the United States prior to the current era of large-scale migration was 1907, when 1.3 million people entered. The recent growth in the immigrant population has been unprecedented. In 1970, the foreign-born population stood at 9.6 million, constituting 4.7 percent of the population. As of 2010, the more than forty million foreign-born represented nearly thirteen percent of the nation's residents.

The United States has experienced sharp downturns in immigration in times of depression and war. Immigration levels fell, for example, during the decade of the U.S. civil war and the Great Depression: 700,000 immigrants entered the United States in the entire 1930s, with a low of 23,000 in 1933.

Assuming net annual migration of 1.2 million persons, the U.S. population is projected to reach 420 million by 2060, compared to 355 million if migration were to cease. It is not hard to understand from Chamie's analysis why population control groups oppose high levels of immigration. It is less understandable why these groups neglect to feature population control arguments in their advocacy. More often, they resort to strained, even specious economic and cultural arguments.

Imperfect and Unsettled Laws

The rule of law enjoys a place of prominence in U.S. civic culture, although this term is often misconstrued to mean "law and order" or zero-tolerance enforcement of the law. This volume offers an historical perspective that highlights imperfect and provisional laws, unsettled in varying degrees, subject to changed conditions, beset by unintended consequences, and in constant need of assessment and regular adjustment. In part, the laws are unsettled because they reflect evolving and hotly disputed understandings of neuralgic issues like national identity, membership, civil rights, federalism, and the rule of law. In addition, the legislative and policymaking process produces (in Wheeler's words) a "mix of cautious first steps to address long-standing challenges and overreactions to perceived threats." In any event, the United States never gets immigration law and policy entirely right.

Nor do lawmakers enjoy a stellar record of anticipating the effect of laws that they pass. As Chamie reports, sponsors of the 1965 Immigration Act argued that the Act would not substantially change U.S. immigration levels or patterns. Yet the law dramatically altered the nation's composition. In 1970, European immigrants accounted for nearly sixty percent of the U.S. foreign-born population, but only 15 percent by the close of the twentieth century. Visas designed to increase U.S. diversity are now open to nationals of almost all European countries. As Wheeler observes, "the region of the world that used to comprise almost all of the foreign-born in the United States is now being encouraged to immigrate in order to 'diversify' the U.S. population."

Opponents of comprehensive immigration reform (CIR) legislation argue that it would repeat the mistakes of IRCA and fail to stem illegal immigration.[2] The volume offers a more nuanced explanation for the growth of the unauthorized population from the 1990s through 2007. It explains that IRCA left substantial numbers of persons without status, did not cover the spouses and children of those who had legalized, and did not account for the needs of employers for temporary workers.[3] As a result, in the 1990s through 2007, the United States experienced large-scale illegal entries by migrants who overwhelmingly found work during periods of low unemployment.

Heightened border enforcement, combined with restrictive legislation like the *Illegal Immigration and Immigrant Responsibility Act of 1996* (IIRIRA), which Wheeler correctly characterizes as the most restrictive immigration law in the last seventy years, has perversely led unauthorized persons to remain in the United States out of fear they will not be able to return if they leave.

An experienced legal practitioner, Wheeler recognizes the central role of Congress in appropriating funds to implement laws and of administrative agencies in interpreting and carrying them out. In cases of disfavored laws or functions (like labor standards enforcement), Congress appropriates wholly insufficient amounts. In the case of immigration enforcement, it has regularly appropriated more funding than the Executive Branch has requested or could accommodate.

---

2 CIR generally refers to legislation that would reform the legal immigration system, legalize a substantial percentage of the unauthorized, and effectively enforce the law.

3 The volume uses the terms "unauthorized," "undocumented" and "irregular" to describe persons without immigration status. For factual reasons, it uses the term "illegal" to describe activity that violates the law (e.g., "illegal entries"), but not to characterize immigrants themselves.

The laws frequently lag behind not only the needs of the nation, but the ingenuity of those who seek to evade them. As Wheeler puts it, the "wretched, the homeless, and the huddled masses," as well as the "strong, the enterprising, and the industrious," have regularly been able to "find ways around" law.

Given their complexity, importance to the national interest, and the volatility of migration push and pull factors, immigration laws and policies should be regularly reviewed and, if necessary, modified. Yet the U.S. legal immigration system has not been substantially revised since 1990 or overhauled since 1965. In addition, Congress has resisted legislative proposals to build flexibility into the admissions process in response to changed conditions and needs.

National Identity and Membership

U.S. immigration laws reflect radically different visions of national identity and membership. Some have nativist roots. The first federal immigration law, the 1790 Naturalization Act, restricted U.S. citizenship to "free white" persons. Chinese laborers began to arrive in large number in the 1850s, and contributed most of the labor, as well as substantial expertise, for the construction of the transcontinental railroad in the 1860s. While the Chinese Exclusion Acts (beginning in 1882) have received significant scholarly attention, more than 30 years earlier the United States prohibited the Chinese, African-Americans and Native Americans from testifying against white persons. The *Immigration Act of 1924,* also known as the Quota Act, sought to freeze the national origin composition of the country as it existed at the time. Racial bars to naturalization were not removed until the mid-twentieth century and national origin remained a basis for exclusion, most notably targeting those from Asia and Mexico, until 1965.

Immigrants have often been seen as a threat in times of war and insecurity. In 1798, President John Adams signed into law the Alien Sedition Acts in response to fears of an invasion by France, the presence of enemy infiltrators, and potential spillover violence from the French revolution. These laws granted the President near absolute authority to arrest, detain and remove aliens from enemy nations and broadly criminalized expressions of opposition to the government. They laid the groundwork for the so-called "plenary power" legal doctrine, which provides that the political branches of government possess broad, nearly unfettered authority to regulate immigration. They also set the precedent for addressing security threats through immigration policy, as occurred with the relocation and internment of U.S. citizens of Japanese descent during World War II and with several excessive security-related measures following the terrorist attacks of September 11, 2001.

On the other hand, some laws have prioritized the integration of diverse groups of immigrants, consistent with a more expansive sense of the national interest. The *Homestead Act of 1862*, for example, encouraged western settlement by making land grants to immigrants that filed a declaration of intent to naturalize. The 1980 Refugee Act created the formal U.S. refugee resettlement program which seeks to integrate refugees through early employment. The colonies were largely formed by settlers seeking religious freedom, and the United States has from its earliest days offered refuge to immigrants fleeing religious persecution, famine (the Irish in the late 1840s), and revolution (the Germans following 1848). The *Displaced Persons Act of 1948* led to the admission of 400,000 Eastern European refugees. Since the fall of Saigon in 1975, the United States has resettled nearly 3 million refugees, most of them from Vietnam, Laos and Cambodia.[4]

Enforcement Growth and Push Back

Just as immigration has always been a feature of the U.S. experience, so too has immigration enforcement. Wheeler finds historical antecedents in colonial laws to modern-day exclusion, deportation, and border enforcement policies. A Delaware Colony law in 1740, for example, precluded admission of the aged, disabled, low-income, and those with a "mental disorder." Ship captains were required to pay a fine and post a bond for transporting persons that had committed certain crimes: bonds could be released if the "immigrant demonstrated good behavior."

Wheeler tracks the collection of passengers' names on ship manifests 300 years ago, to the extensive screening of immigrants (today) against massive immigration, criminal and national security databases. Record-keeping, inspection, head taxes, policing of borders, and the regulation of immigration passed from the colonies to the U.S. states after independence. As late as 1882, immigration regulatory authority was still divided between the federal government and states, which handled day-to-day administration of immigration laws. It was not until the early twentieth century that the federal government assumed jurisdiction over naturalization applications. Wheeler

---

4 War often leads to immigration by foreign nationals that supported the U.S. war effort or were displaced by conflict. It can also lead to preferential immigration treatment for non-citizen U.S. soldiers and their families.

provides a superb description of the way in which tighter enforcement has led to demand for more enforcement tools, more legal authorities, more secure documents, and more programs to address new ways to subvert the law. The Quota Act of 1924, for example, required the United States to capture identity and national origin information for admission. In the current era, employer verification has led to a perceived need for secure national identification cards, with biometric features.

Upwardly spiraling deportations and enforcement funding have characterized the U.S. immigration system for the last quarter of a century. In 1990, the United States deported 30,000 persons. In its first five years, the Obama administration deported roughly two million people, at a rate of nearly 1,100 per day. In 1990, the Immigration and Naturalization Service (INS) received a $1.2 billion appropriation from Congress. By 2012, appropriations to two of the INS successor agencies, the Department of Homeland Security's (DHS) Customs and Border Protection (CBP) and Immigration and Customs Enforcement (ICE), had risen to $17.6 billion. Moreover, funding for these two agencies does not cover immigration enforcement programs that operate in other DHS agencies and divisions, or the substantial enforcement costs borne by non-DHS federal agencies, the federal court system, or states and localities.

This volume also reports on the substantial push-back against and unintended consequences of enforcement. The passage of Proposition 187 in California in 1994 paved the way for state "attrition through enforcement" legislation in the first decade of the twenty-first century.[5] However, Proposition 187 also contributed to making California a reliably Democratic state. Similarly, the federal enforcement build-up has led to a political backlash and the creation of robust immigrant-led coalitions whose members have a substantial stake in reform of the immigration system.

Many have accused the Obama administration of overreaching and even lawlessness in creating the Deferred Action for Childhood Arrivals program (DACA) program and for otherwise exercising its executive authority to

---

5 Proposition 187 sought to bar unauthorized immigrants from virtually all public benefits and services, including primary and secondary education to children. "Attrition through enforcement" refers to a legal strategy that seeks to force immigrants to "self-deport" by denying them the means to subsist.

prioritize enforcement decisions.[6] Wheeler identifies two types of discretion: discretion explicitly built into adjudication and release determinations (as in granting bond to detained immigrants or "humanitarian parole" for those seeking temporary admission) and the discretion inherent in law enforcement agencies in deciding how to enforce the law with limited resources. He finds that executive discretion "dates back to the first federal statutes and to the inherent authority of law enforcement agencies to determine how best to use their limited resources." Enforcement also requires discretion because it invariably implicates other values, like family unity and social cohesion.

The Rise of Civil Society

Campos details the growing sophistication, diversity and influence of civil society on both sides of the U.S. immigration debate. In mapping U.S. civil society in immigration policymaking and service provision, she outlines the work of national advocacy organizations; state, regional and local coalitions; business and labor entities; faith-based institutions; ethnic and community-organizing groups; hometown associations; border networks; advocates for women and children; think tanks; academic centers; foundations and philanthropists; and communications and media organizations. Civil society comprises large, multi-faceted institutions like the Catholic Church with strong immigrant roots and a longstanding commitment to pro-immigrant advocacy and services, as well as effective, nimble, community-based agencies like the National Day Laborer Organizing Network. Collectively, these entities battle before Congress, the Executive Branch and in the federal courts; in cities and states; and in the court of public opinion. They work on issues as consequential as federalism, national identity and citizenship. They also provide substantial legal, resettlement and integration services.

Campos and Wheeler point out that immigration alliances and positions do not divide along standard liberal and conservative lines. Pro-enforcement positions may be espoused by racists and xenophobes. However, they can also be driven by economic, social cohesion, environmental and labor standards concerns. Increased immigration, in turn, may be favored for humanitarian, religious, or "purely capitalistic" reasons.

Campos charts watershed moments in the rising influence of civil society

---

6   DACA provides a quasi-legal temporary status, protection from deportation, and work authorization to certain unauthorized residents who were brought to the United States as children.

on immigration. The qualified designated entities that assisted applicants to legalize under IRCA evolved post-IRCA into a sophisticated national network of charitable legal programs. State and local immigration coalitions, which began to emerge in the 1980s and 1990s, have helped to ground national advocacy in local, grassroots concerns. The Sanctuary movement in the 1980s and the *American Baptist Churches* class action litigation (filed in 1985 and settled in 1991) challenged the biased treatment of Central American refugees. Pro-immigrant foundations assumed a major role in expanding and coordinating immigrant rights and integration initiatives. The DREAMers' counter-intuitive tactic of publicizing their own lack of status has confronted the nation with the anomalies and irrationality of the U.S. immigration system.[7] Civil society responded to the House's passage of restrictionist legislation with perhaps the largest set of civil rights rallies in U.S. history. On the other side of the ideological spectrum, Numbers USA orchestrated an estimated one million calls and faxes that led to the defeat of CIR legislation in 2007.

In June 2013, the Senate passed the *Border Security, Economic Opportunity, and Immigration Modernization Act* (S. 744), but the beginning of the second session of the 113th Congress found the nation at an impasse over immigration reform. Although the immigration debate remains unsettled, it is certain that civil society actors will continue to assert themselves on all sides of the immigration issue in the foreseeable future.

The Need for Regular Assessment and Reform of U.S. Immigration Laws

The election of President Barack Obama to a second term was widely attributed to the overwhelming support he received from minority and immigrant communities. Seventy-one percent of Hispanics, seventy-three percent of Asian Americans, and a majority of Cuban-Americans voted for Obama. Obama's failure to deliver CIR in his first term represented a substantial disappointment to immigrant communities. At the same, the President enjoyed support for championing CIR and for creating the DACA program. By contrast, Governor Romney adopted an immigration platform that consisted of a commitment to "self-deportation" strategies, a promise to end the DACA

---

7 DREAMers is an acronym for the potential beneficiaries of the Development, Relief, and Education for Alien Minors (DREAM) Act, which would legalize unauthorized persons who were brought to the United States as children and who meet residency, good moral character, educational, military service, and other criteria.

program, and only vague rhetorical support for legal immigration.

Many Members of Congress and the press have criticized S. 744 for its alleged unwieldiness, arrogance and micro-management. Advocates have argued that it would legalize too few persons and would continue the massive border enforcement build-up, while neglecting ports-of-entry, which can be more easily exploited by criminals and terrorists. Despite its imperfections and whatever its future, S. 744 might also be seen as a good-faith effort to address the diverse issues, needs, and concerns of the various stakeholders in the immigration system. As Campos puts it, the bill "reflects the diverse, multiple interests" of groups that favor reform.

This volume makes the case that immigration is neither a panacea nor a cause of every social problem. Rather, well-designed, competently-managed, rights-respecting laws can contribute to the national interest, broadly defined to encompass economic well-being and adherence to core civic values. They can also improve the life prospects of migrants and contribute to the development of sending communities. That said, even the most effective laws will need constant assessment and regular reform. As this volume illustrates, lawmakers should not make illusory "perfect" proposals the enemy of good (but imperfect) reforms, or set impossibly high expectations for legislation.

CHAPTER I

International Migration
Trends and Perspectives for the United
States of America

Joseph Chamie

Introduction

The landing of Christopher Columbus in the Western Hemisphere nearly 525 years ago launched an era of massive waves of migration to the Americas initially from Europe and later from Africa and Asia (Zolberg 2006; Hansen 1940; Livi Bacci 2010). At the time of Columbus' arrival, the lands throughout the Americas, including those that would become the United States, were not empty as is often popularly thought, but were inhabited by various indigenous groups who are believed to have their origins from Asia more than a millennium earlier (Barbieri and Quellette 2012; Haines and Steckel 2000). Although difficult to establish accurately due to limited data, rough estimates of the total number of pre-Columbian peoples in the Americas range from 50 million to 100 million (Taylor 2002).

The estimates of the population of the pre-Columbian people living roughly in the territory of the current United States vary widely, but may have been as high as 10 million (Lord 1997). Five centuries later, after enormous voluntary, indentured, forced and refugee immigration, the U.S. population, which was a couple of million at the time of the nation's birth in 1776, has grown rapidly and today stands at 318 million (Table 1). With continuing immigration—currently more than one million per year—the U.S. population is expected to reach approximately 400 million by mid-century and is projected to be approaching a half billion by the end of the twenty-first century (United Nations 2011). The purpose of this chapter is to provide a brief account of historical trends, current levels and future perspectives on international migration to the United States.

1. Historical Trends

Following the landing of Columbus in 1492, the exploration and colonization of the Americas by European powers revolutionized both sides of the Atlantic. The first Europeans, led by the Spanish and French, carried out expeditions and established settlements and outposts in what would become the United States.

One of the first major expeditions occurred when the conquistador Juan Ponce de Leon landed in Florida in April 1513. Ponce de León was later followed by other Spanish explorers, such as Panfilo de Narvaez in 1528 and Hernando de Soto in 1539. The subsequent European colonists to North

America often operated under the belief that they were saving pagans with Western civilization (Spring 2001).

Table 1	Population of the United States 1492 - 2100
Year	Population
1492	~ 10 million*
1620	500**
1640	27 thousand
1660	70 thousand
1680	152 thousand
1700	251 thousand
1720	466 thousand
1740	906 thousand
1760	1.6 million
1770	2.1 million
1776	2.5 million
1780	2.8 million
1790	3.9 million
1800	5.3 million
1850	23 million
1900	76 million
1950	152 million
2000	282 million
2013	318 million
2050	401 million
2100	462 million

Source: Lord 1997; United Nations 2013; U.S. Decennial Census Bureau Reports 1790-2010.
* Total population north of Rio Grande.
** Colonial population until 1776; afterwards U.S. population.

In addition to human migration across the Atlantic, flora and fauna were transported between Europe and the Americas (Tallant 1998). New World animals, such as turkeys, llamas, alpacas and guinea pigs, and plants, such as maize, potatoes, tobacco, peanuts, tomatoes and avocados, were shipped to Europe. And Old World animals, such as sheep, pigs, and cattle, and plants, such as rice, wheat, oats, coffee, olives and dandelions, were introduced to the Native Americans.

Also, Spaniards brought horses to the Americas, which greatly impacted many Indian societies and culture. Some horses escaped and began breeding and growing in numbers in the wild. A number of Indian tribes trained and used horses to ride, to carry packs, to hunt bison and to wage war. Indians, especially those of the Great Plains, fully incorporated the use of horses into their societies and expanded their economies and territories.

By the close of the fifteenth century, the migration of Europeans to the Americas and the forced importation of Africans as slaves resulted in centuries of conflict between the American Indians and those of European origins. The European immigration impacted the Indian societies greatly, causing enormous social, health and cultural disruption, environmental and economic destruction as well as periodic armed conflicts and wars.

Especially noteworthy, the Indian tribes experienced high mortality from infectious Eurasian diseases, such as smallpox, measles, chicken pox, malaria and yellow fever, to which they had little or no immunity. For example, smallpox killed 90 percent of the Indians in 1618–1619, in the area of the Massachusetts Bay (Koplow 2003). Also, historians believe many Mohawk (in present-day New York) became infected with smallpox after contact with the children of Dutch traders in 1634, spreading to the Onondaga by 1636 and the Iroquois by 1679 (Keesler 2004). The spreading epidemics from European contact brought about not only the greatest numbers of death among the indigenous peoples but also produced disruptions and breakdowns in Indian societies and cultures (Livi Bacci 2008; Lord 1997; Keesler 2004).

As the U.S. population expanded westward from the eastern coastline, immigrants came into growing conflict with various Indian tribes, especially nomadic tribes. The Indians strongly resisted European immigrant expansion into their territories. Over time, the United States forced treaties and land cessions upon the Indians and established reservations for them to reside in. The U.S. government also encouraged Indians to assimilate and adopt European life styles and culture. Those Indians who had not already acquired U.S. citizenship were granted citizenship by the U.S. Congress in 1924.

At the start of the seventeenth century, England, France, Spain and the Netherlands initiated various colonization programs in eastern Northern America (Andrews 1914). In 1607, the British established their first permanent outpost in Jamestown in the colony of Virginia. Perhaps most well-known colonial immigration event concerns the voyage of the *Mayflower*. The famous ship set sail in 1620 with about 100 English colonists who came in search of freedom to practice their faith—commonly referred to as the "Pilgrims"— and landed and established a colony in Plymouth, Massachusetts (Philbrick 2006). This historic event is widely considered to be the "start" of planned immigration from Europe to the United States. With the invaluable assistance of the native Indians, the first winter for the Pilgrims also gave rise to the first and uniquely American national holiday, Thanksgiving Day. Following the Pilgrims' colony at Plymouth, the Puritans, approximately 20,000 immigrants arriving from 1630 to 1634, established the Massachusetts Bay Colony.

Subsequently, many European ships arrived in the colonies with various other immigrants, including trappers, traders, adventurers, farmers and indentured servants (Hansen 1940). During the seventeenth century, it is estimated that approximately 175,000 Englishmen migrated to Colonial America (Horn 1996). Many immigrants were too poor to pay for the trip across the Atlantic and indentured themselves to wealthier colonialists for a number of years. An estimated one-half or more of the white Europeans who made the voyage during the seventeenth and eighteenth century arrived as indentured servants. While some voluntarily indentured themselves, others were forced into servitude and thousands of English convicts were sent as indentured servants (Barker, n.d.; Galson 1981; Wilson and Northcott 2008; Zolberg 2006).

In addition to voluntary and indentured European immigration to the colonies along the eastern American coast, the forced migration of West Africans against their will also occurred (Walsh 2000). The earliest records of slavery in the territory that would become the United States include a group of approximately 20 Africans who in 1619 were forced into indentured servitude in Jamestown, Virginia, to aid in the production of such lucrative crops as tobacco (History 2013).

By 1680, it is estimated that there were some 7,000 African slaves in the American colonies (Table 2). Also around that time, and following a number of bloody conflicts, the colonists had enslaved native Indians and sent them to work in Caribbean plantations. In 1676, for example, one of several New England ships, the *Seaflower*, set sail to the West Indies with 180 native Indian slaes (Philbrook 2006).

Slavery was practiced throughout the American colonies in the seventeenth and eighteenth centuries with the African-American slaves helping to establish the economic foundations of the new nation (Curtin 1969; Miller and Smith1988; Steckel 2000). During the seventeenth century, some 21,000 African slaves were forcefully brought from West Africa to the colonies (Table 3).

Table 2.   U.S. African Free and Slave Population: 1790-1860

Year	Total	Free	Slave	Total	Free	Slave
1620	...					
1640	603					
1660	3,000					
1680	7,000					
1700	28,000					
1720	69,000					
1740	150,000					
1760	326,000					
1790	757,208	59,527	697,681	100%	8%	92%
1800	1,002,037	108,435	893,602	100%	11%	89%
1810	1,377,808	186,446	1,191,362	100%	14%	86%
1820	1,771,656	233,634	1,538,022	100%	13%	87%
1830	2,328,642	319,599	2,009,043	100%	14%	86%
1840	2,873,648	386,293	2,487,355	100%	13%	87%
1850	3,638,808	434,495	3,204,313	100%	12%	88%
1860	4,441,830	488,070	3,953,760	100%	11%	89%

Source: Lord 1997; U.S. Decennial Census Bureau Reports 1790-1860.

Table 3. Slaves Imported into United States

Years	Slaves
1620–1700	21,000
1701–1760	189,000
1761–1770	63,000
1771–1790	56,000
1791–1800	79,000
1801–1810	124,000
1810–1865	51,000
Total	597,000

Source: Miller and Smith 1988.

The slave ships traveling from Africa to the Americas had to endure extremely difficult and unhygienic conditions. Many of the ships transported hundreds of slaves, who were chained to their wooden plank beds. Dehydration, dysentery, scurvy and poor nutrition resulted in high mortality rates. More than one in seven captive African slaves perished at sea, with death rates considerably higher in Africa during the process of capturing and transporting indigenous peoples to the ships (Mancke and Shammas 2005). The total number of African deaths directly attributable to the Atlantic slave trade voyages is estimated at up to two million, with African deaths directly related to the institution of slavery from 1500 to 1900 being up to four million (Rosenbaum 2001).

By the start of the nineteenth century, the African-American population in the colonies had grown to one million, with nearly 90 percent of them being slaves (Table 2). Although the U.S. Congress outlawed the importation of slaves in 1808, the practice of slavery continued, especially among the southern states. By the middle of the nineteenth century, the overall number of imported African slaves was nearly 600,000 and the total number of slaves residing in the United States had grown to nearly four million, with an additional half million African-Americans being free (History 2013). The U.S. Civil War resulted in the emancipation of American slaves and in 1865 the Government abolished slavery with the passage of Thirteenth Amendment to the U.S. Constitution.

The colonial populations grew at relatively rapid rates throughout the second half of the eighteenth century due to high birth rates—averaging eight or more births per woman—and comparatively low death rates (Haines 2004; Gerhan and Wells 1989; Smith 1972). In the early years of the United States, immigration was fewer than 8,000 people a year, including French refugees from the slave revolt in Haiti (Weisberger 1994). Immigration played a secondary demographic role at that time until around 1820 when large scale European gradually increased. Some historians estimate that less than a million immigrants, and possibly as few as 400,000, sailed across the Atlantic during the seventeenth and eighteenth centuries (Damon 1981).

With continuing European immigration to the British colonies and high rates of natural increase, the European population in the United States grew rapidly, reaching approximately 275,000 at the beginning of the eighteenth century, with Boston with 7,000 inhabitants as the largest city, followed by New York at 5,000 (Taylor 2013). At the time of the signing of the U.S. Declaration of Independence, on July 4, 1776, the estimated number of people residing in the newly independent nation—the former 13 British colonies—

was about 2.5 million (U.S. Census Bureau 2006), with the large majority being of English, Irish, Scottish or Welsh descent.

The French Revolution also generated additional immigrants to America near the close of the eighteenth century. The new French immigrants lived mainly along the Eastern sea coast, in cities such as Charleston, New York, Baltimore, and Philadelphia, as well as in New Orleans, which later became U.S. territory with the Louisiana Purchase in 1803. The most numerous non-English-speaking immigrants in the United States at the time of independence were Germans. After the Irish immigrants, Germans constituted one of the largest immigrant groups throughout the first half of the nineteenth century.

The first U.S. population census mandated by the newly adopted Constitution was conducted in 1790 and estimated the resident population at 3.9 million. Also in the same year, the U.S. Congress passed the *Naturalization Act of 1790*, which stipulated that "any alien, being a free white person, may be admitted to become a citizen of the United States."

The nineteenth century brought about rapid population growth in America, which was particularly the result of the new immigration of first predominantly Irish, British and Germans followed by large waves of Italians and Russians (Table 4). Although immigration through much of the nineteenth century did not attain the historic high levels that it reached near the close of that century, economic opportunities in the United States attracted many immigrants, who settled new regions and contributed to the development of the country's infrastructure (Gibson and Lennon. 1999).

In addition to the economic opportunities and demand for labor pulling many immigrants to the newly independent nation, economic hardships, social problems and political disorders in many European nations pushed many to America. One of the most significant events impacting U.S. immigration was the Great Irish Famine of 1845-1851, the result of a devastating potato blight. At that time, the Irish were the dominant immigrant group and the famine forced many more to migrate to America. Also, in various German states— which were not united until 1871—a series of failed revolutions in 1848 created a large wave of political refugees to the United States (Bankston 2010).

The year 1820 is the first year for which detailed immigration statistics are available for the United States. Over the subsequent nearly two hundred years, the numbers of U.S. immigrants—those obtaining lawful permanent resident

Table 4. Persons Obtaining Legal Permanent Resident Status to the United States from All Countries, Germany, Italy, Mexico, Russia and United Kingdom: 1820-2012.

Period	All countries	Germany	Ireland	Italy	Mexico	Russia	United Kingdom
1820-29	128,502	5,753	51,617	430	3,835	86	26,336
1830-39	538,381	124,726	170,672	2,225	7,187	280	74,350
1840-49	1,427,337	385,434	656,145	1,476	3,069	520	218,572
1850-59	2,814,554	976,072	1,029,486	8,643	3,446	423	445,322
1860-69	2,081,261	723,734	427,419	9,853	1,957	1,667	532,956
1870-79	2,742,137	751,769	422,264	46,296	5,133	34,977	578,447
1880-89	5,248,568	1,445,181	674,061	267,660	2,405	173,081	810,900
1890-99	3,694,294	579,072	405,710	603,761	734	413,382	328,759
1900-09	8,202,388	328,722	344,940	1,930,475	31,188	1,501,301	469,518
1910-09	6,347,380	174,227	166,445	1,229,916	185,334	1,106,998	371,878
1920-29	4,295,510	386,634	201,644	528,133	498,945	61,604	342,762
1930-39	699,375	117,736	28,195	85,053	32,709	2,473	61,813
1940-49	856,608	119,403	15,701	50,509	56,158	605	131,794
1950-59	2,499,268	576,905	47,189	189,061	273,847	453	195,709
1960-69	3,213,749	209,616	37,788	200,111	441,824	2,329	220,213
1970-79	4,248,203	77,142	11,461	150,031	621,218	28,132	133,218
1980-89	6,244,379	85,752	22,210	55,562	1,009,586	33,311	153,644
1990-99	9,775,398	92,207	65,384	75,992	2,757,418	433,427	156,182
2000-09	10,299,430	122,373	15,642	28,329	1,704,156	167,152	171,979
2010-12	3,136,296	20,813	4,657	8,299	427,946	26,019	40,238
Total	78,493,018	7,303,271	4,798,630	5,471,815	8,068,095	3,988,220	5,464,590

Source: U.S. Department of Homeland Security 2012.

status and those who were naturalized—grew rapidly and varied greatly depending on the economic, social and political circumstances in the country at the time as well as those in the various sending countries (Figures 1 and 2).

The summary statistics in Table 5 present the top five immigrant sending countries for each decade from 1820 to 2012. In addition, the single top sending country for each of those decades is illustrated in Figure 3. During the 1820s, the largest number of arriving immigrants (40 percent) came from Ireland. After the Irish, the immigrants from the United Kingdom (England, Scotland and Wales) were the second largest with 20 percent. Together about 60 percent of all the U.S. immigrants in the 1820s were from the British Isles. The next largest groups were the French (six percent), Germans (four percent) and interestingly Mexicans (three percent), who do not appear among the top five sending nations until about a hundred years later.

Immigration quadrupled during the 1830s, from a total of 128,502 arrivals in the period 1820-29 and 538,381 during 1830-39 (Table 5). New arriving immigrants came from a wide variety of European countries, but most of the 1830s expansion was driven by a dramatic growth in arrivals from Ireland and Germany.

The 1840s saw yet another surge in the tide of European immigrants, with 1,427,337 newcomers reaching U.S. shores during the decade. This figure was almost triple the number of the 1830s and twelve times as large as the number of immigrants during the 1820s. The most important source of new immigrants was again Ireland, which alone represented 46 percent of new immigrants to America. After Ireland, the next highest sending countries were Germany, 27 percent, and the United Kingdom, 15 percent (Table 5).

U.S. immigration continued to increase rapidly during the 1850s, with the number doubling over the previous decade to 2,814,554. Again, Ireland, Germany and the United Kingdom were the top three immigrant sending countries, together accounting for close to 90 percent of the immigrants during this decade (Table 5).

The 1850 census was the first to collect data on the nativity of the population (Gibson and Lennon 1999). These data compiled on a decennial basis permit an analysis of trends in the numbers and proportions of the foreign-born among the U.S. population (Figures 4 and 5). In 1850 the approximate number of foreign-born residing in America was 2.2 million or nearly 10 percent of the total population. Over the subsequent decade the number of foreign-born

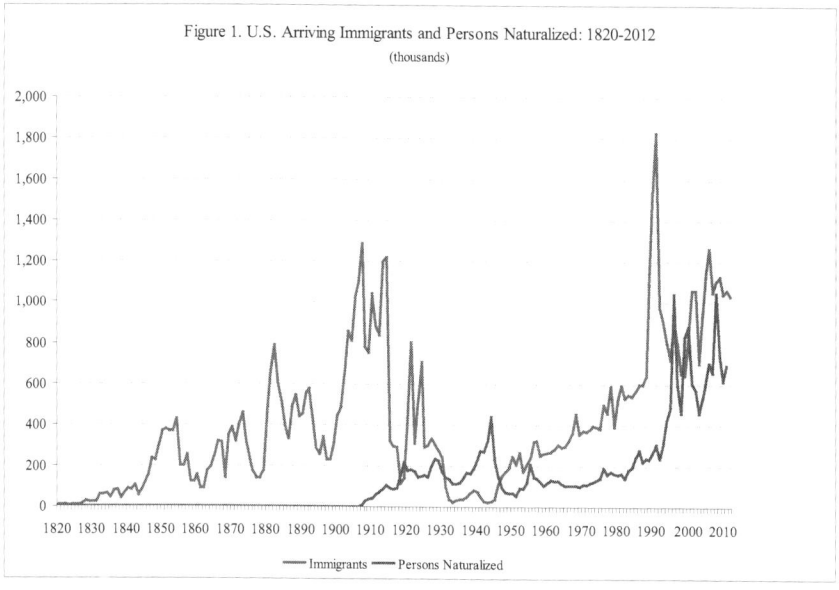

Source: U.S. Department of Homeland Security 2012.

Source: U.S. Department of Homeland Security 2012.

nearly doubled to 4.1 million, representing 13 percent of the country's resident population. The growth of the U.S. foreign-born population continued to increase, more than doubling to 10 million near the close of the nineteenth century and represented 14.8 percent of the total population, which remains a historic high for the United States.

During the decade of the 1860s, when the American Civil War occurred, the number of arriving immigrants declined to 2.1 million. Also, Germany took over the lead from Ireland with their arriving immigrants for that decade representing 35 percent of the total, with the United Kingdom and Ireland following with 26 percent and 21 percent, respectively. Among the top five immigrant-sending countries a notable new entry was China, which accounted for three percent or 54,000 immigrants.

The first large-scale waves of U.S. immigrants from China started when California's Gold Rush began in 1848. Difficult conditions in China at the time, including civil war, famine and lack of employment, pushed many to migrate to the United States, where they found gainful work in mines, agriculture and factories and could send monies back to their families in China (Lowell 1996). Chinese immigrants were particularly instrumental in building the transcontinental railroad in the American west (Behnke 2005).

As was the case for many of the early immigrants to America, the Chinese encountered hostilities, discrimination and restrictions (Pfaelzer 2007). An 1850 U.S. law, for example, prohibited Chinese—as well as Indians and African Americans—from testifying in court against a white person. As the numbers of Chinese immigrant laborers increased, so did the strength of anti-Chinese sentiment among other U.S. workers and their elected officials. This finally resulted in the first law limiting the admission of new immigrants to the United States, the 1982 Chinese Exclusion Act. From 1882 until the end of 1943, when Chinese exclusion acts were repealed, the U.S. Government severely curtailed Chinese immigration (Hipsman and Meissner 2013).

Although the level of U.S. immigration during the 1870s increased by about one third over the previous decade to 2.7 million, the pattern of immigrant-sending countries remained essentially unchanged. Five countries contributed about four-fifths of all the immigrants to the United States in that decade. Germany led with 27 percent, followed by the United Kingdom at 21 percent and Ireland and Canada at 15 percent and 12 percent, respectively. The proportion arriving from China nearly doubled to five percent, with the

Table 5. Persons Obtaining US Legal Permanent Resident Status and Percent for Top Five Sending Countries: 1820-2012.

1820-29		1830-39		1840-49		1850-59	
Total	128,502	Total	538,381	Total	1,427,337	Total	2,814,554
Ireland	40%	Ireland	32%	Ireland	46%	Ireland	37%
U.K.	20%	Germany	23%	Germany	27%	Germany	35%
France	6%	U.K.	14%	U.K.	15%	U.K.	16%
Germany	4%	France	7%	France	5%	France	3%
Mexico	3%	Canada	2%	Canada	2%	Canada	2%
Sum	74%	Sum	78%	Sum	96%	Sum	92%

1860-69		1870-79		1880-89		1890-99	
Total	2,081,261	Total	2,742,137	Total	5,248,568	Total	3,694,294
Germany	35%	Germany	27%	Germany	28%	Italy	16%
U.K.	26%	U.K.	21%	U.K.	15%	Germany	16%
Ireland	21%	Ireland	15%	Ireland	13%	Russia	11%
Canada	6%	Canada	12%	Canada	9%	Ireland	11%
China	3%	China	5%	Sweden	8%	U.K.	9%
Sum	89%	Sum	81%	Sum	73%	Sum	63%

1900-09		1910-19		1920-29		1930-39	
Total	8,202,388	Total	6,347,380	Total	4,295,510	Total	699,375
Italy	24%	Italy	19%	Canada	22%	Canada	23%
Russia	18%	Russia	17%	Italy	12%	Germany	17%
Hungary	8%	Canada	11%	Mexico	12%	Italy	12%
Austria	6%	Austria	9%	Germany	9%	U.K.	9%
U.K.	6%	Hungary	9%	U.K.	8%	Mexico	5%
Sum	62%	Sum	66%	Sum	63%	Sum	66%

1940-49	
Total	856,508
Canada	19%
U.K.	15%
Germany	14%
ico	7%
Italy	6%
Sum	61%

1950-59	
Total	2,499,268
Germany	23%
Canada	14%
Mexico	11%
U.K.	8%
Italy	8%
Sum	64%

1960-69	
Total	3,213,749
Mexico	14%
Canada	13%
U.K.	7%
Germany	7%
Cuba	6%
Sum	47%

1970-79	
Total	4,248,203
Mexico	15%
Philippines	8%
Cuba	6%
Rep. Korea	6%
Canada	4%
Sum	39%

1980-89	
Total	6,244,379
Mexico	16%
Philippines	8%
Rep. Korea	5%
India	4%
Dom. Rep.	4%
Sum	37%

1990-99	
Total	9,775,398
Mexico	28%
Philippines	5%
Russia	4%
Dom. Rep.	4%
India	4%
Sum	45%

2000-09	
Total	10,299,430
Mexico	17%
China	6%
India	6%
Philippines	5%
Dom. Rep.	3%
Sum	36%

2010-12	
Total	3,136,296
Mexico	14%
China	8%
India	7%
Philippines	6%
Dom. Rep.	5%
Sum	38%

Source: Author's calculations based on U.S. Census Bureau Decennial Reports and U.S. Department of Homeland Security Yearbooks of Immigration Statistics.

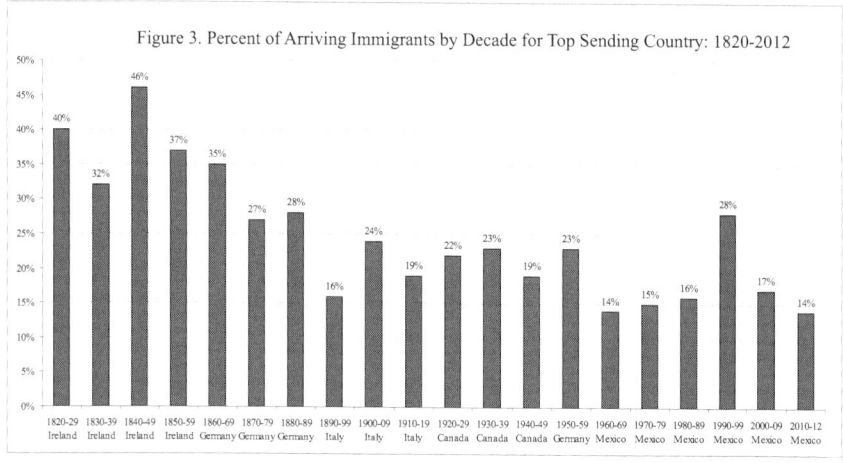

Source: U.S. Department of Homeland Security 2012.

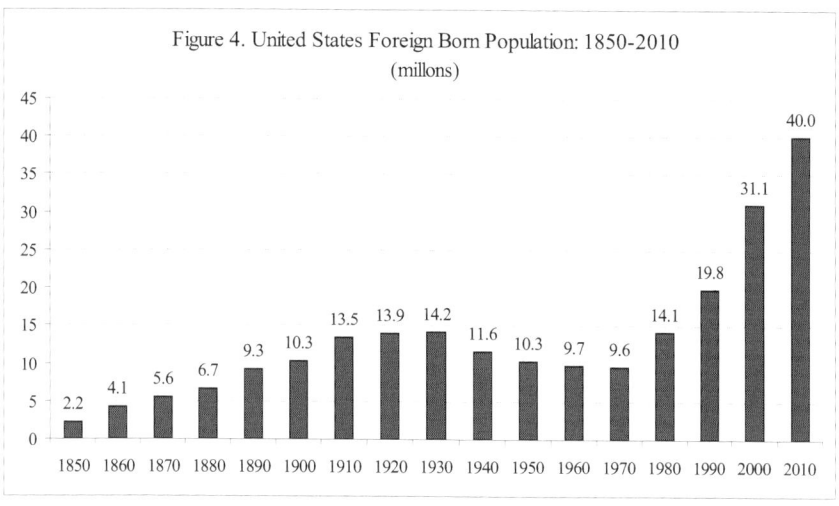

Source: Gibson and Yung 2006; Grieco et al. 2012.

numbers growing from 54,000 in the previous decade to 133,000. However, the surge in Chinese immigration during the 1870s was short lived. As noted earlier, beginning in 1882, the Chinese exclusion acts significantly restricted the number of U.S. immigrants coming from China.

With the rapid economic expansion of the country and growing demand for labor, immigration again nearly doubled during the 1880s, with 5.3 million immigrants arriving in that ten-year period, which would be the highest decennial immigration level of the nineteenth century. The top five sending countries remained unchanged except that immigration from China declined precipitously, experiencing a 90 percent decline, and was replaced by Sweden in fifth place (Table 5).

Although the top sending countries for nearly 80 years were Ireland and Germany, with the United Kingdom in third place, this ordering changed markedly in the last decade of the nineteenth century (Figure 6). The top sending country to the United States during the 1890s was Italy, accounting for 16 percent of all immigrants (Figure 3). In addition, Russia moved to third place among the sending countries with 11 percent of the immigrants.

By the close of the nineteenth century nearly 20 million people had immigrated to the United States during the 100 year period (Table 5). Although less than half of the number of immigrants arriving in America during the twentieth century, the impact of nineteenth century immigration on the new nation was considerable given that the country was rapidly expanding westward and the total population was considerably smaller, e.g., 23 million in 1850 versus 151 million in 1950.

As a result of a slowdown in the American economy near the century's end, the numbers of immigrants during the 1890s declined by 1.6 million to 3.7 million. However as it turned out, this decline in immigrant numbers was again short-lived. The first decade of the twentieth century more than made up for the decline in the previous decade, with 8.2 million immigrants arriving in America, a level not to be seen until the end of the twentieth century (Table 5).

The peak year for admission of new immigrants was 1907, when about 1.3 million people entered the country legally, a high that stood until the large immigration in 1990s (Figure 1). As a consequence of these unprecedented numbers, the 1910 census found that 14.7 percent of the U.S. population was foreign-born, virtually the same as the record high of 14.8 percent reported in the 1890 census (Gibson and Lennon 1999).

Again, immigrants from Italy took the top position, with nearly two million immigrants and accounting for about one-quarter of all immigrants. The

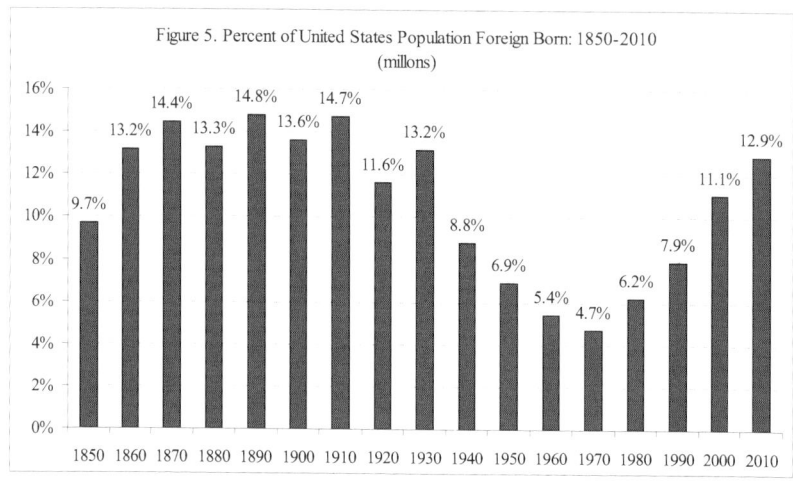

Source: Gibson and Yung 2006; Grieco et al. 2012.

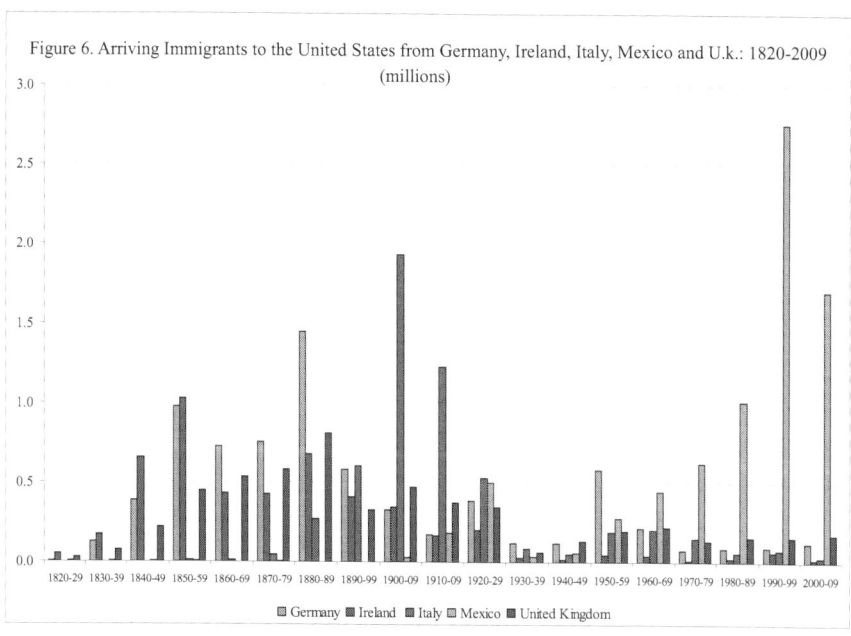

Source: U.S. Department Homeland Security 2012.

Russian immigrants advanced to second place with 1.5 million immigrants or nearly one-fifth of total number. Other immigrant sending countries joining the top five were Hungary and Austria with eight percent and six percent, or 686,000 and 532,000, respectively.

Prior to the twentieth century, Italian immigration to the United States was comparatively limited (Figure 7). For example, though most of the nineteenth century the annual number of Italian immigrants was less than one thousand (Cavaioli 2008). Troubled by low wages and high taxes, large numbers of Italians decided to migrate to the America.

During the period 1900-1909, approximately 2.1 million Italian immigrants arrived in America, with the peak year being 1907 when 286 thousand Italians arrived (Figure 7). These early 20th century Italian immigrants came mostly from rural communities in Southern Italy, especially from Sicily, Campania, Abruzzo and Calabria.

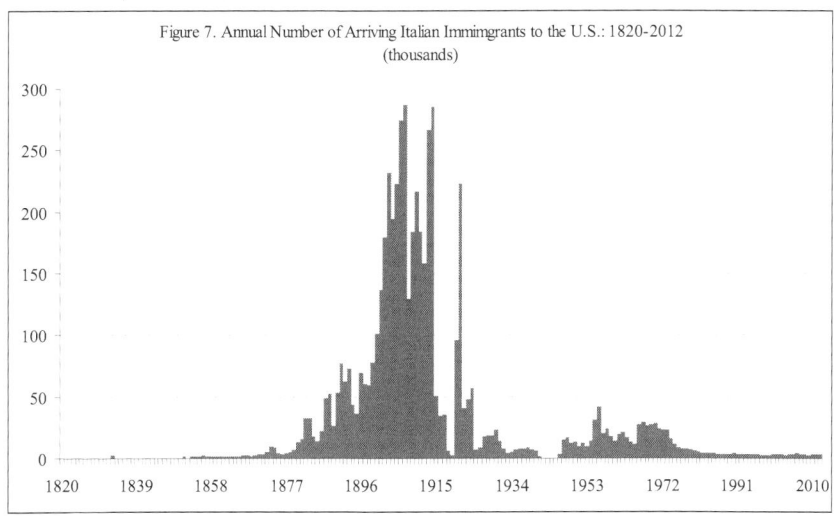

Figure 7. Annual Number of Arriving Italian Immimgrants to the U.S.: 1820-2012 (thousands)

Source: U.S. Department of Homeland Security 1985.

With little or no knowledge of the English language and little education, most Italian immigrants were obligated to accept the lowest paying and least desirable jobs. Many took up unskilled work in U.S. industrial cities, such as New York, Chicago, Philadelphia and Detroit. As was the case for immigrants in the past, Italian immigrants were looked upon as different from the older generations of immigrants and were often viewed as people of lower class. Many newspapers in the early 1900s depicted the Italian as inferior, inept and prone to crime perhaps because many lived in the worst areas of the towns where they settled and not infrequently experienced discrimination.

Also, the Italian immigrants, like numerous immigrants before them, were willing to work long hours at low wages and began to rival the Irish immigrants for much of the unskilled work available in industrial areas. Again, as often had been the case with other immigrant groups, this rivalry would at times lead to hostilities and skirmishes between the two groups of immigrant workers.

While in the first half of the second decade of the twentieth century 11 million Italian immigrants arrived in the United States, the number in the second half fell to 125 thousand immigrants due to World War I. Italian immigration rebounded in the early years following the war with nearly a quarter million arriving in 1921 alone. However, this surge lasted only for a few years, with the number of Italian immigrants falling to about six thousand in 1925. The large waves of Italian immigration to the United States was largely over; even following World War II, the annual numbers would be well below 30 thousand (Figure 7).

In addition to the decline in immigration due to World War I, Congress enacted legislation requiring immigrants over 16 to pass a literacy test, and in the early 1920s immigration quotas were established. The *Immigration Act of 1924* created a quota system that restricted entry to two percent of the total number of people of each nationality in America as of the 1890 national census – a system that favored immigrants from Western Europe – and prohibited immigrants from Asia.

Immigration continued during the 1920s, but at much lower levels than took place in the previous 20 years. About 4.3 million immigrants arrived in the decade of the 1920s, with the largest group from Canada, accounting for a fifth of the immigrants. Dropping from first place in the previous decade to second position at 12 percent was Italy. Surprisingly among the top five sending countries and closely behind Italy was the re-entry of Mexico, also at approximately 12 percent.

Since 1880, when China dropped off the list, all of the top five sending countries were largely of European origin and Europe was by far the largest source of immigrants to the United States (Figure 8). Also, as will be seen

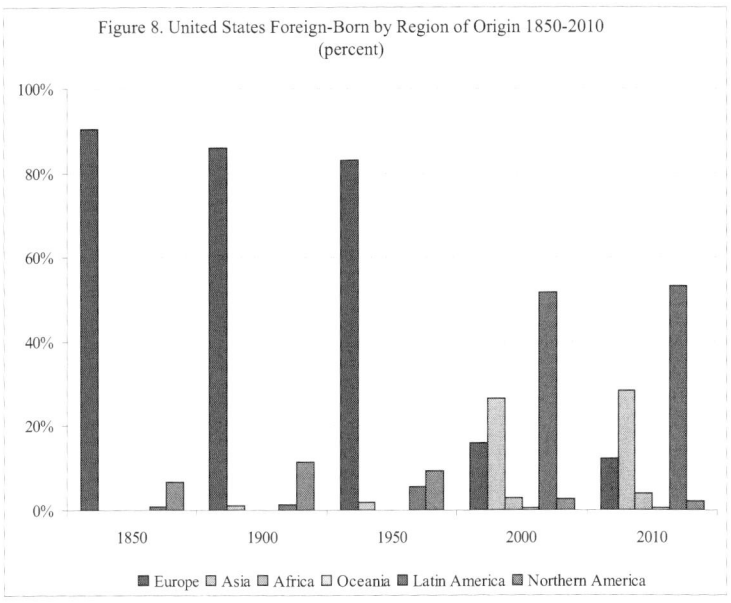

Figure 8. United States Foreign-Born by Region of Origin 1850-2010 (percent)

■ Europe □ Asia ■ Africa □ Oceania ■ Latin America ■ Northern America

Source: Gibson and Yung 2006; Grieco et al. 2012.

later, not only did Mexico rejoin the group of top five sending countries, but beginning in the 1960s America's southern neighbor became and, by a large margin, now represents the largest immigrant sending country to the U.S.

With the collapse of the U.S. stock market and the start of the Great Depression, immigration to the United States declined precipitously and continued to decline over ten years. In 1929, the final year of the roaring twenties, 280 thousand U.S. immigrants arrived, compared to only 23 thousand in 1933, which since 1883 remains an historic low (Figure 1). The number of immigrants during the 1930s turned out to be the lowest for the twentieth century, nearly 700 thousand for the entire decade. The number of immigrants would continue to remain low, not exceeding one hundred thousand annually, until 1946.

It is also noteworthy that in the early 1930s, more people emigrated from the United States than immigrated to it (Hanke 2008). The American government established a Mexican repatriation program that encouraged Mexican immigrants to return home, but thousands are reported to have been involuntarily deported (Thernstrom 1980). It is estimated that about 400 thousand Mexicans were repatriated (Bryant 1998). Also, a few decades later, during the 1950s, the American Government launched Operation Wetback, which deported about one million Mexicans in 1954 (Navarro 2005).

2. Recent Trends

Following the Second World War, the number of U.S. immigrants began to increase again, but slowly and usually no more than a few hundred thousand a year until the late 1960s, when the annual number was approaching one half million (Figure 1). As a result of the comparatively low levels of immigration during the 1930s and 1940s, the foreign-born population in America declined from 14.2 million in 1930 to 10.3 million in 1950 (Figure 4), or from 13.2 percent to 6.9 percent of nation's population (Figure 5). The foreign-born population continued to slowly decline, dropping to 9.7 million in 1960 and 9.6 million in 1970, when it hit an historic record low 4.7 percent of the total population.

During the 1950s, the top immigrant sending country was Germany, accounting for nearly a quarter of the 2.5 million immigrants arriving in America in that decade (Table 5). Canada and Mexico followed Germany with 14 percent and 11 percent, respectively. The other countries among the top five were the United Kingdom and Italy, both at around eight percent. As was clearly the case during earlier decades, the overwhelming majority of U.S. immigrants continued to have European origins (Figure 8).

Also following World War II, the United States began differentiating between immigrants and refugees and established policies and programs that treated them separately. The country decided to provide refuge to persons who have been persecuted or have a well-founded fear of persecution through two programs: one for refugees (persons outside the United States and their immediate relatives) and one for asylees (persons in the United States and their immediate relatives). One year after legally being granted asylum or refugee status in the United States, the person may apply to become a lawful permanent resident and eventually an American citizen. Today refugees compose about one-tenth of the total annual immigration to the United States.

The first refugee legislation in the United States was the *Displaced Persons Act of 1948,* which brought 400,000 Eastern Europeans to the United States, including Hungarian refugees from Hungary's failed revolt against Soviet control. Up until the middle of the 1990s, refugees for the most part arrived from the former Soviet Union and Southeast Asia, in particular Vietnam.

In the three decades between 1950 and 1980, various refugee-related bills were adopted by Congress, culminating in the *Refugee Act of 1980*. The 1980 Act attempted to harmonize the U.S. refugee definition and standards with international law, e.g., the 1951 Convention relating to the Status of Refugees and its 1967 Protocol. The 1980 Act provides a systematic procedure for the admission to the United States of refugees of special humanitarian concern to the United States, and comprehensive and uniform provisions for the effective resettlement and absorption of those refugees who are admitted (Akner and Posner 1981; Batalova 2011; Kennedy 1981).

The Refugee Act differentiates between refugee and asylum status and allows certain refugee applicants to be processed while in their countries of nationality. Also, before the beginning of each fiscal year, the U.S. president, in consultation with Congress, establishes an overall refugee admissions ceiling as well as regional allocations. The ceiling for refugee admissions in 2011 was 80,000 and the largest regional allocation was to the Near East/South Asia region, which accounted for 44 percent of the total ceiling (Martan and Yankay 2012).

Since 1980, 2.6 million refugees from all over the world have arrived in America (Table 6 and Figure 9). The peak year was 1980 with 207,106 refugee arrivals. The annual figures have remained below 100,000 since 1995, with the most recent year, 2011, having 56,384 refugee arrivals. For the last several years, the top 10 refugee sending countries account for at least 90 percent of the total, with three countries, Iraq, Bhutan and Myanmar, contributing about two-thirds of all refugee arrivals (Table 7).

In contrast to other forms of immigration, asylum has no quotas or limits on number of visas. Persons requesting asylum need to demonstrate a "well-founded fear" of persecution in his or her home country. In the last few years, the number of asylum seekers accepted into the United States was no more than 25,000 (Table 8). In 2011, the number of asylees to the United States was 24,988, an increase of several thousand over 2010. In recent years, the United States has accounted for 15-20 percent of all asylum-seeker acceptances in the Organization for Economic Co-operation and Development (OECD) countries (OECD 2012).

In 2011, the leading countries of nationality of persons granted asylum were China (34 percent), Venezuela (4.4 percent), Ethiopia (4.3 percent), Egypt

(4.1 percent), and Haiti (3.5 percent) (Table 8). Together these five countries accounted for half of all persons granted asylum (Gibson and Yankay 2012).

Table 6. Refugees Arrivals to United States: 1980-2011

Year	Number
1980	207,116
1981	159,252
1982	98,096
1983	61,218
1984	70,393
1985	67,704
1986	62,146
1987	64,528
1988	76,483
1989	107,070
1990	122,066
1991	113,389
1992	115,548
1993	114,181
1994	111,680
1995	98,973
1996	75,421
1997	69,653
1998	76,712
1999	85,285
2000	72,143
2001	68,925
2002	26,788
2003	28,286
2004	52,840
2005	53,738
2006	41,094
2007	48,218
2008	60,107
2009	74,602
2010	73,293
2011	56,384

Source U.S. Department of Homeland Security 2012

In addition to establishing new policies and programs for refugees following World War II, Congress also began reviewing legislation concerning immigration levels, trends and composition. Up until the mid-1960s, various laws and the quota system favored European immigration. During the 1950s, for example, three countries—Germany, Italy and the United Kingdom—continued to be major sending countries to America, accounting for 40 percent of all immigrants in that decade (Table 5).

In 1965, with the adoption of the *Immigration and Nationality Act*, also known as the Hart-Cellar Act, the system of national origin quotas that for many decades had restricted immigration from non-European countries was abolished. Notable pronouncements and assurances by sponsors of the Actmaintained that U.S. cities would not be flooded with a million immigrants annually, the country's ethnic mix would not be upset and the ethnic immigration patterns would not change sharply (United States Senate 1965).

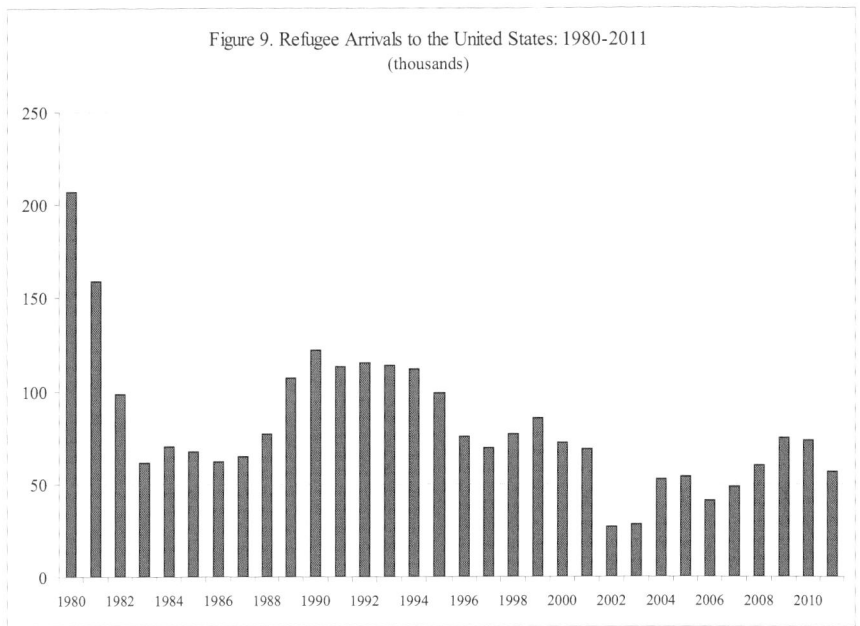

Figure 9. Refugee Arrivals to the United States: 1980-2011
(thousands)

Source: U.S. Department Homeland Security 2012.

However, contrary to those and other assurances, the 1965 Act did in fact result in higher levels of immigration, exceeding a million annually in recent years. Also, immigration increased markedly from non-European countries, such as Mexico, China, India, the Philippines and the Dominican Republic. Whereas European immigrants accounted for nearly 60 percent of the total foreign population in 1970, by the close of the twentieth century the European proportion declined to 15 percent (Figure 8). In addition, the 1965 Act changed the nation's ethnic composition, particularly giving rise to a rapidly increasing proportion of the population having Latin American ancestry.

Also during the 1960s, the numbers of arriving immigrants were substantially greater than the previous decade, averaging around 300,000 per year. Moreover, in sharp contrast to the trends of past decades, the top sending country was no longer a European nation, but was now Mexico, which continues to maintain this position to the present day.

Over the closing decades of the twentieth century, the numbers of immigrants to the United States increased rapidly (Figure 1). Whereas during the 1960s decade the number of arriving immigrants was 3.2 million, the number more than tripled to 9.8 million during the last decade of the twentieth century. In addition, the largest annual total in the country's history occurred in 1991 with 1,826,595 immigrants.

That record decade, however, was surpassed during the first decade of the twenty-first century, with 10.3 million U.S. immigrants (Table 5). Furthermore, there were nearly eight million U.S. immigrants between 2000 and 2005, the highest of any five-year period in U.S. history. (El Nasser and Kiely 2005, Kandel 2011, Washington Times 2005).

In 1970, the proportion of the U.S. foreign-born population fell to its historic lowest point, 4.7 percent. Since then, due to large-scale immigration mainly from Latin America and Asia, the proportion and number of foreign-born have grown rapidly. By 2010, the number of U.S. foreign- born was at an all-time high of 40 million (Figure 4), or nearly 13 percent of the country's population (Elmendorf 2013) (Figure 5). The 2010 U.S. immigrant population is twice as large as it was in 1990, three times that of 1980 and four times that of 1970, when it was estimated at 9.6 million immigrants.

As emphasized in the earlier section, most of the nearly 78 million U.S. immigrants arriving over the last two centuries came from European nations. Throughout the decades of the nineteenth century and the first half of the twentieth century, the major immigrant sending countries were Germany, Italy the United Kingdom and Ireland (Table 5).

Table 7.   Number and Percent of Refugee Arrivals to the United States from Top Ten Sending Countries: 2007–2011

Country	2007 No.	2007 Percent	2008 No.	2008 Percent	2009 No.	2009 Percent	2010 No.	2010 Percent	2011 No.	2011 Percent
Total	48,218	100%	60,107	100%	74,602	100%	73,293	100%	56,384	100%
Burma	13,896	29%	18,139	30%	18,202	24%	16,693	23%	16,972	30%
Bhutan	-	0%	5,320	9%	13,452	18%	12,363	17%	14,999	27%
Iraq	1,608	3%	13,822	23%	18,838	25%	18,016	25%	9,388	17%
Somalia	6,969	14%	2,523	4%	4,189	6%	4,884	7%	3,161	6%
Cuba	2,922	6%	4,177	7%	4,800	6%	4,818	7%	2,920	5%
Eritrea	963	2%	251	0%	1,571	2%	2,570	4%	2,032	4%
Iran	5,482	11%	5,270	9%	5,381	7%	3,543	5%	2,032	4%
Congo, D.R.	848	2%	727	1%	1,135	2%	3,174	4%	977	2%
Ethiopia	1,028	2%	299	0%	321	0%	668	1%	560	1%
Afghanistan	441	1%	576	1%	349	0%	515	1%	428	1%
Sum	34,157	71%	51,104	85%	68,238	91%	67,244	92%	53,469	95%

Source: U.S. Department of Homeland Security 2012.

Table 8.   Number and Percent of Asylees to the United States from Top
Ten Sending Countries: 2009-2011

Country	2009		2010		2011	
	Numbe	Percent	Number	Percent	Number	Percent
Total	22,219	100%	21,056	100%	24,988	100%
China	6,159	28%	6,678	32%	8,601	34%
Venezuela	585	3%	648	3%	1,107	4%
Ethiopia	1,111	5%	1,086	5%	1,076	4%
Egypt	482	2%	531	3%	1,028	4%
Hait	1,006	5%	833	4%	878	4%
Nepal	665	3%	638	3%	749	3%
Russia	492	2%	548	3%	663	3%
Eritrea	431	2%	358	2%	640	3%
Columbia	1,005	5%	592	3%	538	2%
Guatemala	508	2%	464	2%	484	2%
Sum	12,444	56%	12,376	59%	15,764	63%

Source: Martin and Yankay 2012.

In contrast, with the passage of the 1965 Immigration Reform Act, most immigrants since 1980 have been arriving from non-European nations (Table 9). Again, clearly the dominant sending country is Mexico, which has contributed about one-fifth of the 28 million arriving immigrants over the past thirty years. The country in second place, which may surprise some, is the Philippines, which accounted for six percent of U.S. immigrants since 1980. Other major immigrant sending countries are India (five percent), China (four percent) and the Dominican Republic (three percent). The only European nation among the top ten immigrant sending countries is the Russian Federation, accounting for two percent of the total.

With the start of the second decade of the twenty-first century, U.S. immigration patterns continue to be similar to those during the closing two decades of the twentieth century. Immigration for the most part is coming from Latin America and Asia (Table 10). Mexico clearly remains the leading immigrant sending country in 2012, accounting for 13 percent of immigrants, followed by China (eight percent), India (six percent), the Philippines (five percent) and the Dominican Republic (four percent) (Monger and Yankay 2013).

Table 9.   Top Ten Immigrant Sending Countries to the United States:
1820-2011 and 1980-2012

	1820-2011			1980-2012	
Country	Number	Percent	Country	Number	Percent
Total	77,461,387	100%	Total	29,455,503	100%
Mexico	7,921,699	10%	Mexico	5,899,116	20%
Germany	7,297,459	9%	Philippines	1,750,834	6%
Italy	5,469,142	7%	India	1,373,591	5%
United Kingdom	5,452,576	7%	China	1,337,687	5%
Ireland	4,797,116	6%	Dominican Republic	1,014,354	3%
Canada	4,746,446	6%	Vietnam	857,482	3%
Austria-Hungary	4,408,836	6%	Rep. Korea	777,852	3%
Russia	3,978,251	5%	El Salvador	714,952	2%
Norway-Sweden	2,183,642	3%	Cuba	665,784	2%
Philippines	2,124,323	3%	Russia	659,909	2%
Sum	48,379,490	62%	Sum	15,051,561	51%

Source: U.S. Department of Homeland Security 2012.

Table 10. Legal Permanent Resident Flows to the United States for Top Ten Countries:
2000, 2011 and 2012

	2000		2011		2012	
Country	Number	Percent	Number	Percent	Number	Percent
Mexico	173,493	20.6%	143,446	13.5%	146,406	14.2%
China	45,585	5.4%	87,016	8.2%	81,784	7.9%
India	41,903	5.0%	69,013	6.5%	66,434	6.4%
Philippines	42,343	5.0%	57,011	5.4%	57,327	5.6%
D. Republic	17,465	2.1%	46,109	4.3%	41,566	4.0%
Cuba	18,960	2.3%	36,452	3.4%	32,820	3.2%
Vietnam	26,553	3.2%	34,157	3.2%	28,304	2.7%
Haiti	21,977	2.6%	22,111	2.1%	22,818	2.2%
Colombia	14,427	1.7%	22,635	2.1%	20,931	2.0%
Korea	15,721	1.9%	22,824	2.1%	20,846	2.0%
US Total	841,002	100.0%	1,062,040	100.0%	1,031,631	100.0%

Source: Monger and Yankay 2013.

The 2010 U.S. immigrant population of 40 million is distributed widely across the nation, but with large concentrations in a handful of states (Table 11). California, for example, contains about 10.2 million immigrants, or about 27 percent of the state's population. Other notable states are New York with 4.3 million immigrants (22 percent of the state population), Texas with 4.1 million (16 percent of the state) and Florida with 3.6 million (19 percent of the state). These four states together contain 56 percent of the U.S. immigrant population.

In 2010 the average age of a U.S. immigrant was 42.4 years compared to 36.6 years for native-born (Camarota 2012, Motel and Patten 2013), although of course the native-born include the children of immigrants. While the proportions for those aged 65 years and older are roughly the same among the foreign-born and native-born (13 percent), notable differences exist among children and those in the working ages (Table 12). For example, whereas about a quarter of the native-born are less than 18 years of age, the corresponding proportion for the U.S. foreign-born is about six percent. In the working ages of 18 to 64, the proportion for U.S. foreign-born is markedly higher than that for the native-born, 80 percent versus 60 percent.

In recent years, the proportions of U.S. immigrant flows aged less than five years and 65 years or more—by and large considered dependents—have been between four and five percent (Table 13). In contrast, about one-fourth of the lawful permanent resident flow has been made up by those in the prime working and reproductive age group 25-34 years (Figure 10). The next highest age groups, each with around 18 percent, are those aged 15-24 years and 35-44 years.

Family-sponsored immigrants, which include the immediate relatives of U.S. citizens as well as family preference classes, account for about two-thirds of the total legal permanent resident flow in 2012 (Table 14). The largest major admission group is the immediate relatives of U.S. citizens (46 percent), consisting of spouses (27 percent), parents (12 percent) and children (eight percent). The other three major admission categories were employment-based (14 percent), refugees and asylees (15 percent) and diversity immigrant class (four percent) (Figure 11).

While every U.S. state has received immigrants, five states accounted for 58 percent of all lawful permanent residents in 2012 (Table 15). California was the clear leader with 19 percent, followed by New York (15 percent), Florida (10 percent), Texas (nine percent) and New Jersey (five percent) (Figure 12).

Table 11. Number and Percent of US Immigrant Population by State: 2010

State	Population	Percent	State	Population	Percent
California	10,150,429	27.2	Utah	222,638	8.0
New York	4,297,612	22.2	South Carolina	218,494	4.7
Texas	4,142,031	16.4	Oklahoma	206,382	5.5
Florida	3,658,043	19.4	New Mexico	205,141	9.9
New Jersey	1,844,581	21.0	Kansas	186,942	6.5
Illinois	1,759,859	13.7	Louisiana	172,866	3.8
Massachusetts	983,564	15.0	Alabama	168,596	3.5
Georgia	942,959	9.7	Kentucky	140,583	3.2
Virginia	911,119	11.4	Iowa	139,477	4.6
Washington	886,262	13.1	Rhode Island	134,335	12.8
Arizona	856,663	13.4	Arkansas	131,667	4.5
Maryland	803,695	13.9	Nebraska	112,178	6.1
Pennsylvania	739,068	5.8	Idaho	87,098	5.5
North Carolina	719,137	7.5	Wash. D.C.	81,734	13.5
Michigan	587,747	6.0	Delaware	1,868	8.0
Nevada	508,458	18.8	New Hampshire	69,742	5.3
Colorado	497,105	9.8	Mississippi	61,428	2.1
Connecticut	487,120	13.6	Alaska	49,319	6.9
Ohio	469,748	4.1	Maine	45,666	3.4
Minnesota	378,483	7.1	Vermont	27,560	4.4
Oregon	375,743	9.8	West Virginia	22,511	1.2
Indiana	300,789	4.6	South Dakota	22,238	2.7
Tennessee	288,993	4.5	Montana	20,031	2.0
Wisconsin	254,920	4.5	North Dakota	16,639	2.5
Hawaii	248,213	18.2	Wyoming	15,843	2.8
Missouri	232,537	3.9	Total	39,955,854	12.9

Source: U.S. Census Bureau 2010.

Table 12. Number and Percent of Foreign Born and Native Born in the United States by Sex and Age: 2011

| | Foreign Born | | | | Native Born | | | |
| | Male | | Female | | Male | | Female | |
Age	Number	Percent of all foreign born	Number	Percent of all foreign born	Number	Percent of all foreign born	Number	Percent of all foreign born
Less than 18	1,330,591	3.3	1,295,341	3.2	36,468,328	13.4	34,756,435	12.8
18 to 64	16,297,263	40.4	16,252,120	40.2	81,246,952	30	82,556,933	30.4
65 and older	2,125,286	5.3	3,080,973	7.6	15,779,568	5.8	20,402,129	7.5
Total	19,753,140	48.9	20,628,434	51.1	133,494,848	49.2	137,715,497	50.8

Source: U.S. Census Bureau 2011.

Table 13. Legal Permanent Resident Flow by Age: 2010-2012

| | 2012 | | 2011 | | 2010 | |
State	Number	Percent	Number	Percent	Number	Percent
Total	1,031,631	100.0%	1,062,040	100.0%	1,042,625	100.0%
Under 5 years	37,495	3.6%	38,378	3.6%	37,592	3.6%
5-14	115,986	11.2%	123,123	11.6%	118,987	11.4%
15-24	189,698	18.4%	199,114	18.7%	191,328	18.4%
25-34	249,111	24.1%	252,917	23.8%	253,188	24.3%
35-44	187,101	18.1%	197,377	18.6%	195,209	18.7%
45-55	117,397	11.4%	120,797	11.4%	118,070	11.3%
55-64	79,206	7.7%	77,198	7.3%	75,817	7.3%
65 +	55,628	5.4%	53,126	5.0%	52,425	5.0%
Median age	31		31		31	

Source: Monger and Yankay 2013.

Table 4. Legal Permanent Resident Flow by Major Admission Category: 2010-2012

Major admission category	2012		2011		2010	
	Number	Percent	Number	Percent	Number	Percent
Total	1,031,631	100.0%	1,062,040	100.0%	1,042,625	100.0%
Family-sponsored immigrants	680,799	66.0%	688,089	64.8%	691,003	66.3%
Immediate relatives of US citizens	478,780	46.4%	453,158	42.7%	476,414	45.7%
Spouses	273,429	26.5%	258,320	24.3%	271,909	26.1%
Parents	124,230	12.0%	114,527	10.8%	116,208	11.1%
Children	81,121	7.9%	80,311	7.6%	88,297	8.5%
Family-sponsored preferences	202,019	19.6%	234,931	22.1%	214,589	20.6%
Unmarried children of US citizens	20,660	2.0%	27,299	2.6%	26,998	2.6%
Spouses & children of alien residents	99,709	9.7%	108,618	10.2%	92,088	8.8%
Married children of US citizens	21,752	2.1%	27,704	2.6%	32,817	3.1%
Siblings of US citizens	59,898	5.8%	71,310	6.7%	62,686	6.0%
Employment-based preferences	143,998	14.0%	139,339	13.1%	148,343	14.2%
Priority workers	39,316	3.8%	25,251	2.4%	41,055	3.9%
Professionals with advanced degrees	50,959	4.9%	66,831	6.3%	53,946	5.2%
Skilled, professional, unskilled workers	39,229	3.8%	37,216	3.5%	39,762	3.8%
Special immigrants	7,866	0.8%	6,701	0.6%	11,100	1.1%
Investors	6,628	0.6%	3,340	0.3%	2,480	0.2%
Diversity programs	40,320	3.9%	50,103	4.7%	49,763	4.8%
Refugees and Asylees	150,614	14.6%	168,460	15.9%	136,291	13.1%
Refugee adjustments	105,528	10.2%	113,045	10.6%	92,741	8.9%
Asylee adjustments	45,086	4.4%	55,415	5.2%	43,550	4.2%
Other categories	15,900	1.5%	16,049	1.5%	17,225	1.7%

Source: Monger and Yankay 2013.

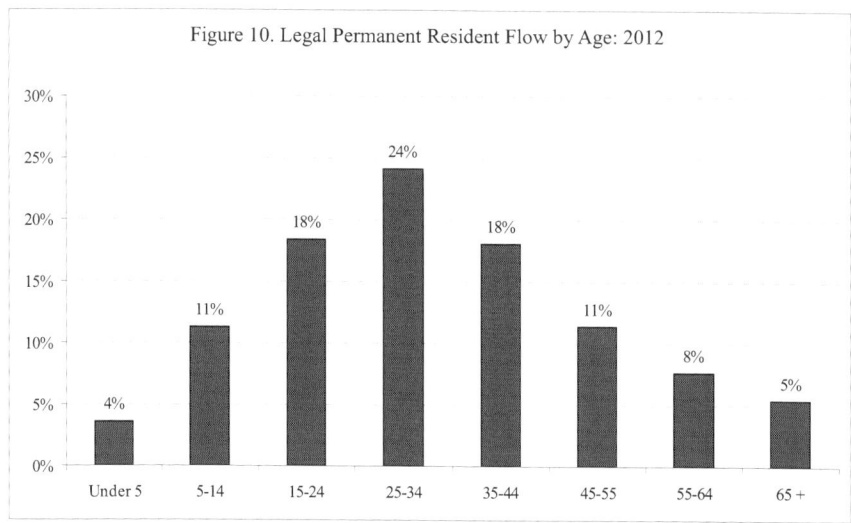

Source: Monger and Yankay 2013.

Table 15. Legal Permanent Resident Flow by State: 2010-2012

	2012		2011		2010	
State	Number	Percent	Number	Percent	Number	Percent
Total	1,031,631	100.0%	1,062,040	100.0%	1,042,625	100.0%
California	196,622	19.1%	210,591	19.8%	208,446	20.0%
New York	149,505	14.5%	148,426	14.0%	147,999	14.2%
Florida	103,047	10.0%	109,229	10.3%	107,276	10.3%
Texas	95,557	9.3%	94,481	8.9%	87,750	8.4%
New Jersey	50,790	4.9%	55,547	5.2%	56,920	5.5%
Illinois	38,373	3.7%	38,325	3.6%	37,909	3.6%
Massachusetts	31,392	3.0%	32,236	3.0%	31,069	3.0%
Virginia	28,227	2.7%	27,767	2.6%	28,607	2.7%
Georgia	26,134	2.5%	27,015	2.5%	24,833	2.4%
Maryland	25,032	2.4%	25,397	2.4%	24,130	2.3%
Other	286,952	27.8%	293,026	27.6%	287,686	27.6%

Source: Monger and Yankay 2013.

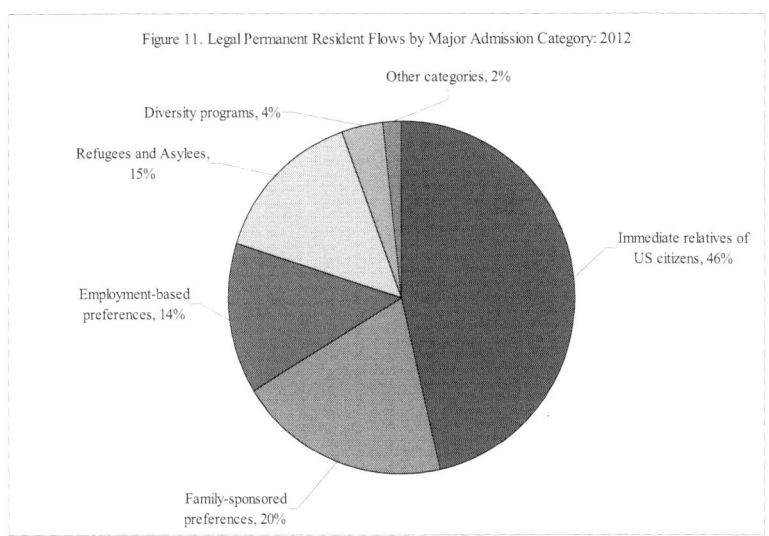

Figure 11. Legal Permanent Resident Flows by Major Admission Category: 2012

Source: Monger and Yankay 2013.

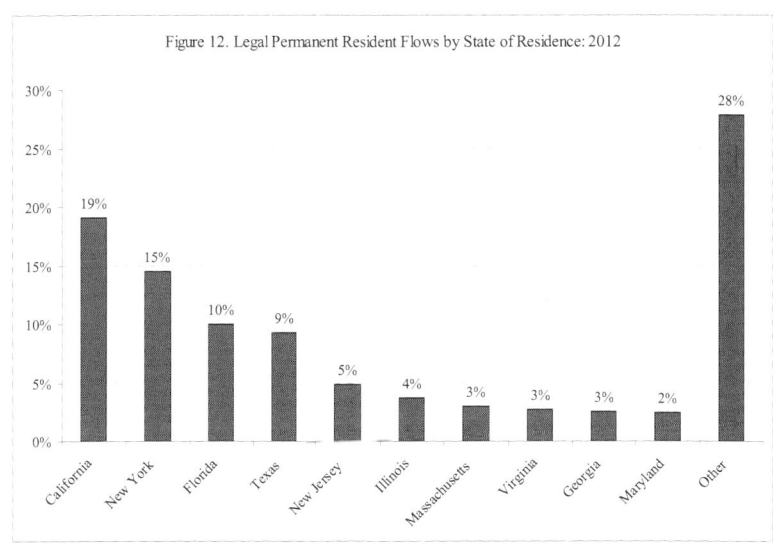

Figure 12. Legal Permanent Resident Flows by State of Residence: 2012

Source: Monger and Yankay 2013.

In addition to legal immigration, the United States has also experienced irregular immigration, especially following World War II, that is, foreigners irregularly crossing the border into the United States as well as others overstaying their lawful visits. In the past, government administrations of both major political parties have attempted to address the issue of irregular immigration through a variety of policies and programs. During the 1950s, for example, President Eisenhower launched "Operation Wetback," a deportation initiative to return Mexicans residing in the United States without immigration status. In addition to the tens of thousands who were caught and sent back to Mexico, hundreds of thousands voluntarily returned to their homeland.

In contrast, three decades following Eisenhower's Operation Wetback, President Reagan signed the 1986 *Immigration Reform and Control Act* (IRCA), which permitted migrants irregularly residing in the country to remain and regularize their legal status. With the intention that this legislation would be the country's last amnesty, IRCA aimed to limit irregular immigration through greater border control, making it illegal to hire unauthorized immigrants, sanctioning employers that did so, and granting legal status to nearly three million unauthorized immigrants who had lived (without status) in the United States for five years and met other conditions, which subsequently could lead U.S. citizenship. Also, following IRCA's adoption, a myriad of legalization programs for smaller populations, but significant in overall total numbers legalized, have been adopted (Kerwin 2010).

Despite the intentions of IRCA and subsequent programs, the numbers of unauthorized persons residing in the United States continued to grow through the closing decade of the twentieth century and into the twenty-first century (Hoefer, Rytina and Baker 2012). By the year 2000, the estimated unauthorized immigrant population in the United States was 8.5 million. The most recent estimate for 2011 puts the unauthorized immigrant population at 11.5 million (Hoefer, Rytina and Baker 2012, Passel and Cohn 2012, Warren and Warren 2013), which is down from its peak of nearly 12 million in 2007 (Figure 13).

Approximately three-quarters of unauthorized U.S. immigrants are from neighboring Latin American countries (Table 16). Mexico, by far the largest contributor to the unauthorized population, accounts for about 60 percent of the total, followed by El Salvador (six percent), Guatemala (five percent) and Honduras (three percent) (Figure 14). Other major origin countries are China, India and the Philippines, each accounting for a quarter million or more unauthorized immigrants.

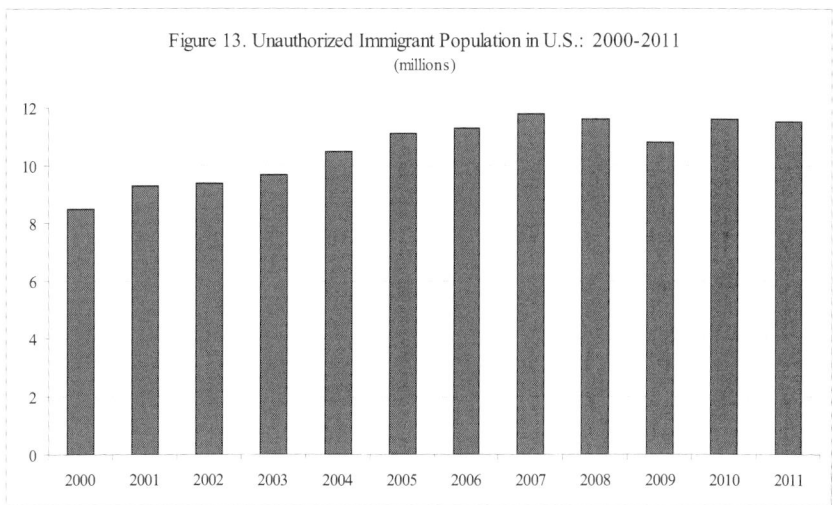

Figure 13. Unauthorized Immigrant Population in U.S.: 2000-2011 (millions)

Source: Hoefer et al. 2012

Table 16. Country of Origin for Unauthorized Immigrant
Population in the United States: 2011

Country	Number	Percent
All countries	11,510,000	100
Mexico	6,800,000	59
El Salvador	660,000	6
Guatemala	520,000	5
Honduras	380,000	3
China	280,000	2
Philippines	270,000	2
India	240,000	2
Korea	230,000	2
Ecuador	210,000	2
Vietnam	170,000	2
Other Countries	1,750,000	15

Source: Hoefer et al. 2012.

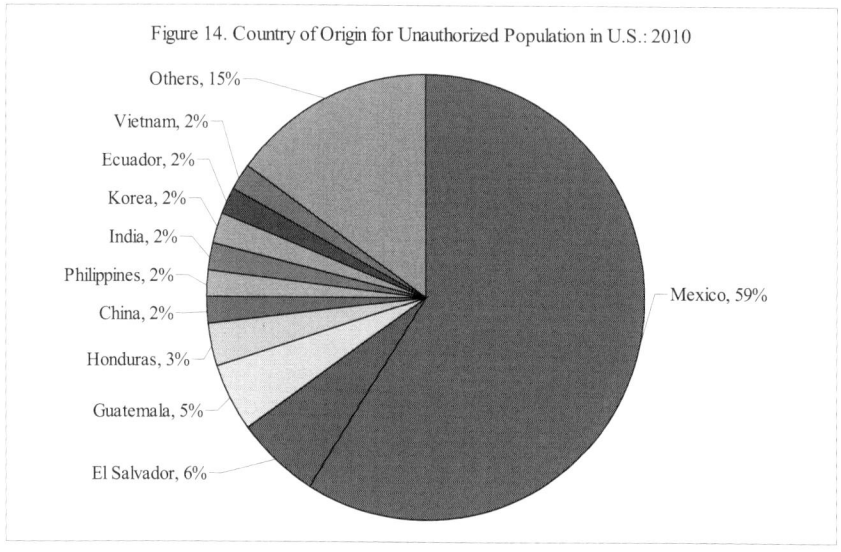

Figure 14. Country of Origin for Unauthorized Population in U.S.: 2010

Source: Hoefer, et al. 2012.

As in the past, the U.S. government is again attempting to address comprehensive immigration reform and in particular the sensitive issue of irregular immigration. Some members of the U.S. Senate are putting forward various ideas, extensive plans and draft bills to overhaul the current immigration system, including a pathway to citizenship for the estimated 11.5 million unauthorized immigrants, increased border security and interior enforcement, reforms to immigrant and non-immigrant visa programs, and immigrant integration provisions (Migration Policy Institute 2013).

3. Future Trends

From its very founding in 1776, immigration has greatly affected the growth, structure and composition of the U.S. population (Barrett, Bogue and Anderton 1997; Carter, et al. 2006). Indeed, the dominant force fueling America's demographic growth is immigration. The underlying reason for this is because immigrants not only add their own numbers to the nation's overall population, but also contribute a significant number of births, whose effects are compounded over time.

Consider, for example, the hypothetical case of what America's population would be today if international migration had ceased after the signing of the Declaration of Independence in 1776, when the colonies numbered approximately 2.5 million people. Assuming the birth and death rates of the past and no immigration after its founding, the current U.S. population would be no more than 143 million, far short of its current size of 318 million (Figure 14). Over this 237 year period, immigration's contribution – migrants and their descendants – accounts for at least 55 percent of America's population growth.

In addition, as noted earlier, immigrants have constituted a significant demographic presence throughout America's history. At the start of the twentieth century, the proportion foreign-born in United States peaked at close to 15 percent. Proportions in many states, however, were considerably higher than the nation's, e.g., California (25 percent), Connecticut (26 percent), Massachusetts (30 percent), Minnesota (29 percent), and New York (26 percent). Today the nation's proportion foreign-born stands at 13 percent, with the lead states being California (27 percent), New York (22 percent), New Jersey (21 percent) and Florida (20 percent).

In the coming decades, immigration will continue to have a dominant demographic impact on the U.S. population. By the year 2060, for example, assuming annual net migration of approximately 1.2 million, the U.S. population is projected to reach about 420 million (Figure 15), or nearly a 33 percent increase (Figure 16). However, if future immigration were to cease, the U.S. population in 2060 would be considerably less, e.g., roughly 355 million or nearly a 12 percent increase (Figure 8). Again, the major force behind the projected growth of America's population, approximately 65 percent in this instance, is the addition of immigrants and their descendants.

Furthermore, in the longer term, if net migration to the United States were to continue at about 1.2 million per year, America's population would be substantially larger by the century's close than is being projected (Chamie 2009). The United Nations, for example, projects a U.S. population of 462 million by 2100, assuming immigration begins declining at mid-century and falls to little more than a trickle by the end of the century. However, if current annual net immigration levels were to remain at approximately 1.2 million, the U.S. population in 2100 would be twice as large as it is today or 632 million (Figure 15).

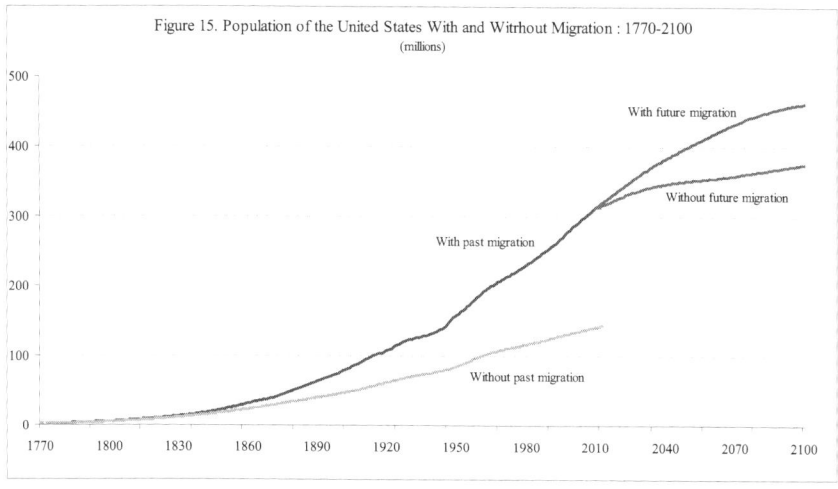

Figure 15. Population of the United States With and Witrhout Migration : 1770-2100
(millions)

Source: U.S. Census Bureau 2012b; United Nations 2013; Chamie 2009.

Beyond its major impact on the size of America's population, immigration also has a significant effect on the country's age structure. Immigrants greatly contribute to the U.S. working age population, thereby increasing the size of the labor force. With slightly more than one million immigrants per year, the U.S. working-age population, ages 20 to 64, is projected to increase by 17 percent by mid-century (Figure 17). However, if immigration to the United States were halted, its working-age population in 2050 would be about one percent smaller than it is today. In addition, without immigration the numbers in the primary working ages would decline substantially while the older age groups would be increasing (Figure 18)

Furthermore, immigration contributes to slowing down the process of population ageing. For example, the proportion of America's population aged 60 years or older in 2050 is projected to be about 25 percent with immigration versus nearly 30 percent without immigration. Clearly, immigration trends have non-trivial implications for the future financial well-being of social security and health care systems for the elderly. However, at the same time, it is important to note that immigration is not a solution to population ageing insofar as the immigrants themselves also age and eventually retire (United Nations, 2000).

In addition, as was shown above, immigration is also altering America's

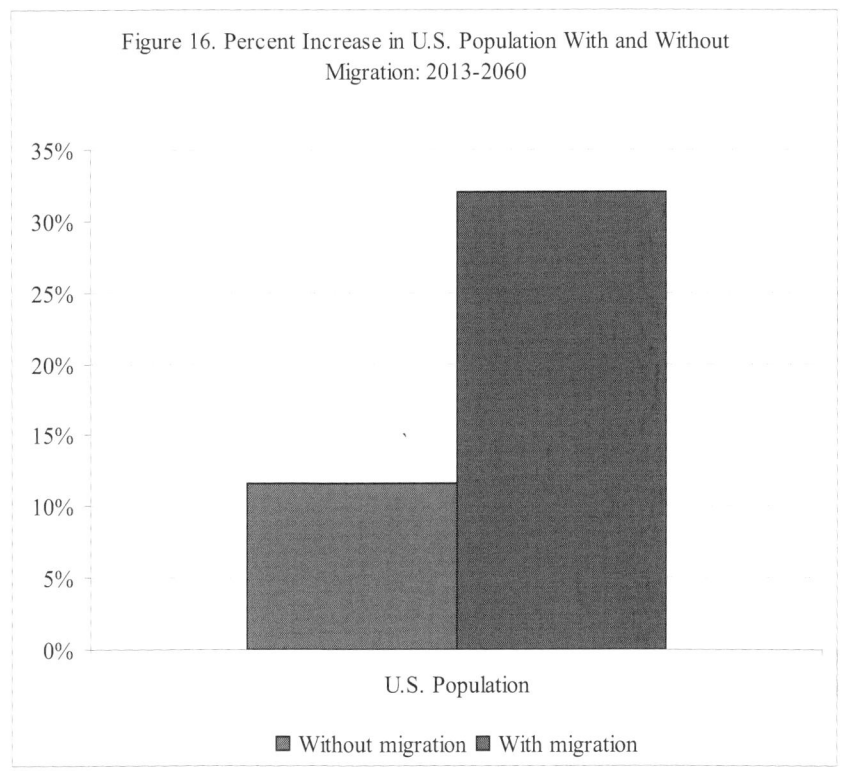

Figure 16. Percent Increase in U.S. Population With and Without Migration: 2013-2060

■ Without migration ■ With migration

Source: United Nations 2013.

ethnic composition and culture, e.g.., less European and more Latin American, Asian and African. Throughout the nineteenth century and most of the twentieth, the U.S. foreign-born population was predominantly from European countries, e.g., Germany, Ireland, Italy and the United Kingdom. These past immigration trends are reflected in the current ethnic composition of the country with Germany at 15 percent of the U.S. population, Ireland at 13 percent, the United Kingdom at 11 percent and Italy at six percent (Table 17).

Today the top five countries are no longer of European origin but are Mexico, China, India, the Philippines and Vietnam, with Mexico accounting for close to 30 percent of the U.S. foreign-born (Table 17). The presence of Mexican immigrants in the United States has increased rapidly over the past few decades (Figure 19). In 2010 the number of Mexican immigrants to the United States was 11.7 million, or close to triple the figure in 1990 (4.3 million) and more than 15 times as large as the number in 1970 (769 thousand). A major factor behind this rapid growth of the Mexican immigrants was unauthorized immigration. Of the nearly 12 million Mexicans residing in the United States, it is estimated that 6.8 million, or about 58 percent, are unauthorized migrants.

Based on recent migration trends and assumptions about future immigration, America will increasingly look, sound and behave differently over the coming decades. For example, whereas in 1960 slightly less than one in twenty Americans was of Hispanic origin, today one in six Americans report Hispanic ancestry. In addition, by 2060 one in five Americans is expected to be an immigrant— the highest level in the past was 14.8 percent in 1890—and those reporting Hispanic ancestry are projected to account for one in three Americans (Figure 20). It should also be noted that as has been the case throughout its history, Americans are not strictly endogamous, with many marrying outside their specific ethnic groups. As a result, in its collection of data on ancestry in the American Community Survey, the U.S. Census Bureau permits people to identify themselves with having more than one ethnic ancestry.

With current demographic trends likely to continue for some time, immigration will certainly have major impacts on the future size, age-structure and ethnic composition of the United States. In addition to those impacts, immigrants are making noteworthy contributions to the labor force and economic growth of the United States and these trends are expected to accelerate if the proposed comprehensive immigration reform is adopted. Also, as recently witnessed following the 2012 national elections, America's political parties and leaders are increasingly recognizing the growing significance of Hispanic voting patterns. This recognition is altering political dynamics as well as past policies and outlooks.

Finally, it should be kept in mind that while the above population projections for America's future may appear likely, they are not necessarily inevitable. Demographic trends may change radically due to behavioral changes and unanticipated events affecting fertility and mortality as well as changes in immigration policies and practices, which as has been the case throughout the nation's history, continues to shape the levels, structure and composition of American immigration.

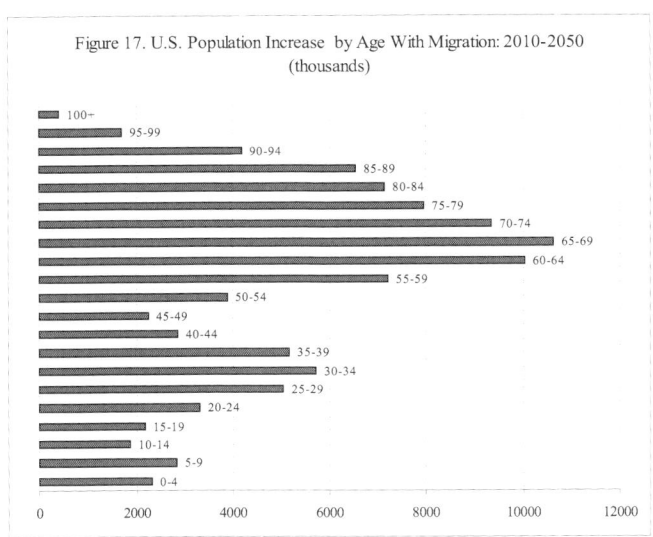

Figure 17. U.S. Population Increase by Age With Migration: 2010-2050 (thousands)

Source: United Nations 2013.

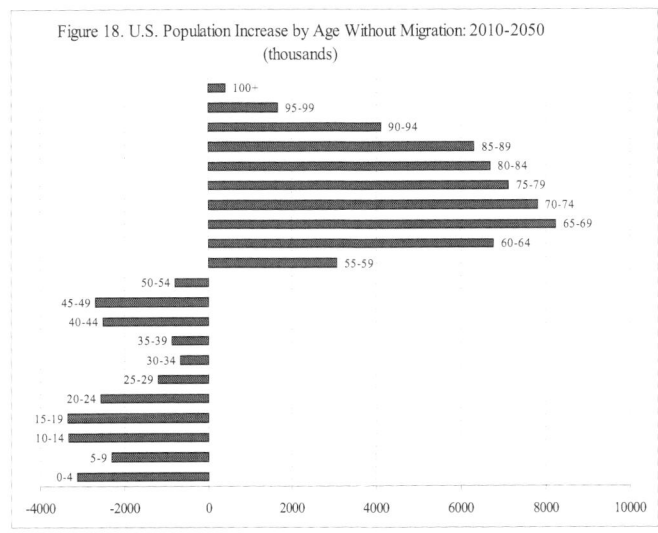

Figure 18. U.S. Population Increase by Age Without Migration: 2010-2050 (thousands)

Source: United Nations 2013.

Table 17. U.S. Population by Ethnicity and U.S. Foreign Born Population by Country of Birth: 2011

Ethnicity by Country	Number	Percent	Foreign Born by Birth Country	Number	Percent
Germany	48,088,000	15.4%	Mexico	11,691,632	29.0%
Ireland	39,285,000	12.6%	India	1,855,705	4.6%
Mexico	34,824,000	11.2%	Philippines	1,814,875	4.5%
United Kingdom	33,243,000	10.7%	China	1,651,511	4.1%
Italy	17,433,000	5.6%	Vietnam	1,253,910	3.1%
Poland	9,472,000	3.0%	El Salvador	1,245,458	3.1%
France	8,635,000	2.8%	Korea	1,095,084	2.7%
Puerto Rico	5,410,000	1.7%	Cuba	1,090,084	2.7%
Netherlands	4,462,000	1.4%	Dominican Republic	878,858	2.2%
China	4,398,000	1.4%	Guatemala	844,332	2.1%
Norway	4,391,000	1.4%	Canada	787,542	2.0%
Sweden	4,036,000	1.3%	Jamaica	694,600	1.7%
Philippines	3,627,000	1.2%	Colombia	655,096	1.6%
India	3,472,000	1.1%	Germany	618,227	1.5%
Canada	3,176,000	1.0%	Haiti	602,733	1.5%
El Salvador	2,271,000	0.7%	Honduras	499,987	1.2%
Cuba	2,121,000	0.7%	Poland	452,224	1.1%
Vietnam	1,999,000	0.6%	Ecuador	429,316	1.1%
Korea	1,825,000	0.6%	Peru	406,008	1.0%
Dominican Republic	1,751,000	0.6%	Russia	398,086	1.0%
Sum	233,919,000	75.0%	Sum	27,776,000	68.8%
US Total Population	311,800,000	100.0%	US Foreign Born Population	40,381,574	100.0%

Source: Motel and Patten 2013 and Migration Policy Institute Data Hub.

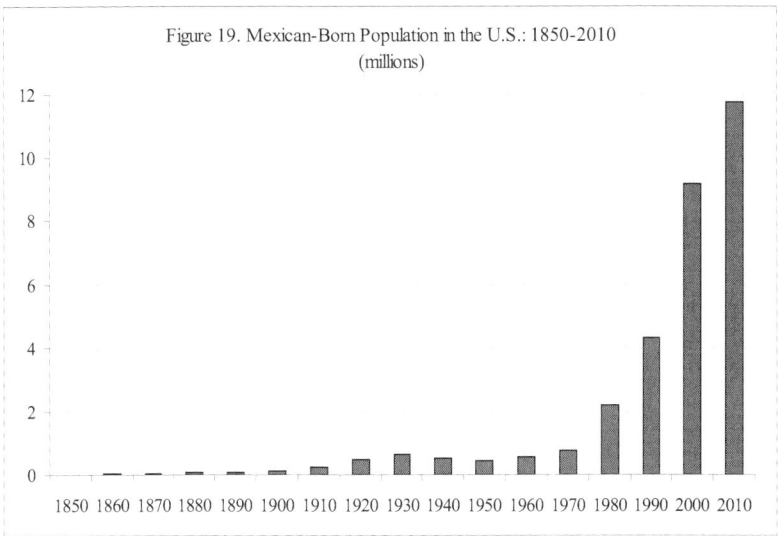

Figure 19. Mexican-Born Population in the U.S.: 1850-2010 (millions)

Source: U.S. Decennial Census Bureau Reports 2000 and 2010; Gibson and Lennon 1999.

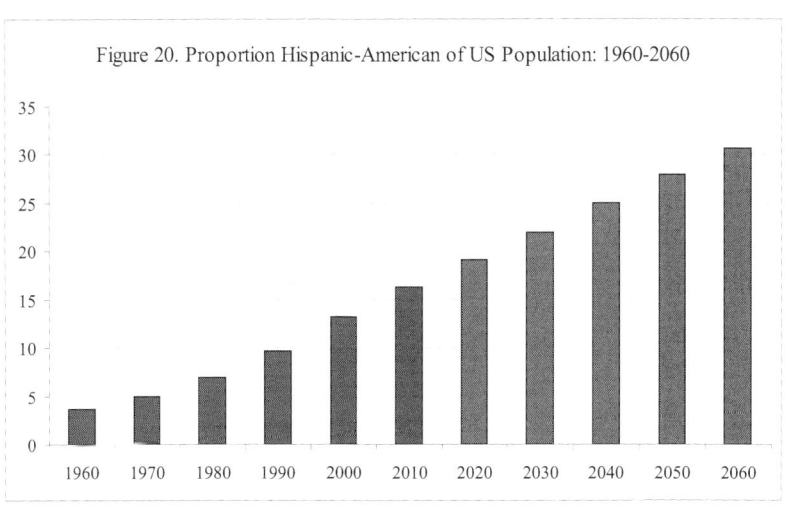

Figure 20. Proportion Hispanic-American of US Population: 1960-2060

Source: U.S. Census Bureau 2012a.

References

Anker, Deborah E. and Michael Posner. 1981. "The Forty Year Crisis: A Legislative History of the Refugee Act of 1980." *San Diego Law Review* 19 (9): 9-89.

Andrews, Charles M. 1914. "Colonial Commerce." *American Historical Review* 20 (1): 43–63.

Bankston, Carl L., ed. 2010. *Encyclopedia of American Immigration.* Hackensack, NJ: Salem Press.

Barbieri, Magali and Nadine Ouellette. 2012. "The Demography of Canada and the United States from the 1980s to the 2000s." English Edition, *Population* 67(2): 177-280.

Barker, Deanna. n.d. "Indentured Servitude in Colonial America." *Frontier Resources.* http://mertsahinoglu.com/research/indentured-servitude-colonial-america/

Barrett, Richard E., Donald J. Bogue and Douglas L. Anderton. 1997. *The Population of the United States,* 3rd ed. New York: The Free Press.

Batalova, Jeanne, and Monica Li. 2011. "Refugees and Asylees in the United States." *Migration Information Source.* Washington, D.C.: Migration Policy Institute.

Bryant, Joyce. 1998. *The Great Depression and New Deal.* Yale-New Haven Teachers Institute. http://www.yale.edu/ynhti/curriculum/units/1998/4/98.04.04.x.html.

Camarota, Steven A. 2012. *Immigrants in the United States, 2010: A Profile of America's Foreign-Born Population.* Washington, D.C.: Center for Immigration Studies. http://www.cis.org/sites/cis.org/files/articles/2012/immigrants-in-the-united-states-2012.pdf

Carter, Susan B., Scott Sigmund Gartner, Michael R. Haines, and Alan L. Olmstead, eds. 2006. *The Historical Statistics of the United States.*

Cambridge: Cambridge University Press.

Cavaioli, Frank J. 2008. "Patterns of Italian Immigration to the United States." *The Catholic Social Science Review* 13: 213-229.

Chamie, Joseph. 2009. "US Immigration Policy Likely to Boost Population." *Yale Global Online,* July 30. http://yaleglobal.yale.edu/content/us-immigration-policy-likely-boost-population.

Curtin, Philip De Armind. 1969. *The Atlantic Slave Trade: A Census.* Madison, WI: University of Wisconsin Press.

Damon, Allan L. 1981. "A Look at the Record: The Facts behind the Current Controversy over Immigration." *American Heritage Magazine* 33(1).

El Nasser, Haya and Kathy Kiely. 2005. "Study: Immigration grows, reaching record numbers." *USA Today,* December 12.

Elmendorf, Douglas W. to Paul Ryan. May 8, 2013. "A Description of the Immigrant Population – 2013 Update." Congressional Budget Office. http://www.cbo.gov/sites/default/files/cbofiles/attachments/44134_Description_of_Immigrant_Population.pdf

Galson, David W. 1981. *White Servitude in Colonial America: An Economic Analysis.* Cambridge: Cambridge University Press.

Gerhan, David R. and Robert V. Wells. 1989. *A Retrospective Bibliography of American Demographic History from Colonial Times to 1983.* Westport, CT: Greenwood Press.

Gibson, Campbell J. and Emily Lennon. 1999. *Historical Census Statistics on the Foreign-born Population of the United States: 1850-1990.* Population Division Working Paper No 29. Washington, D.C.: US Census Bureau. http://www.census.gov/population/www/documentation/twps0029/twps0029.html

Gibson, Campbell and Kay Jung. 2006. *Historical Census Statistics on the Foreign-Born Population of the United States: 1850-2000.* U. S. Census Bureau Population Division Working Paper No. 81.

Washington, D.C.: U. S. Census Bureau.
http://www.census.gov/population/www/documentation/
twps0081/twps0081.pdf

Grieco, Elizabeth M., Edward Trevelyan, Luke Larsen, Yesenia D. Acosta, Christine Gambino, Patricia de la Cruz, Tom Gryn, and Nathan Walters. 2012. *The Size, Place of Birth, and Geographic Distribution of the Foreign-Born Population in the United States: 1960 to 2010.* U.S. Census Bureau Population Division Working Paper No. 96. Washington, D.C.: U.S. Census Bureau.

Haines, Michael. 2004. "Fertility and Mortality in the United States." *EH.net,* http://eh.net/encyclopedia/fertility-and-mortality-in-the-united-states/

Haines, Michael and R.H. Steckel, eds. 2000. *A Population History of North America.* Cambridge: Cambridge University Press.

Hanke, Steve. H. 2008. "A Great Depression." *Globe Asia,* December.

Hansen, Marcus Lee. 1940. *The Atlantic Migration,* 1607-1860: *A history of the continuing settlement of the United States.* Cambridge, MA: Harvard University Press.

Hipsman, Faye and Doris Meissner. 2013. "Immigration in the United States: New Economic, Social, Political Landscapes with Legislative Reform on the Horizon." *Migration Information Source.* Washington, D.C.: Migration Policy Institute.

History. 2013. *Slavery in America.* http://www.history.com/topics/slavery.

Hoefer, Michael, Nancy Rytina and Bryan C. Baker. 2012. *Estimates of the Unauthorized Immigrant Population Residing in the United States: January 2011.* Office of Immigration Statistics Policy Directorate. Washington, D.C.: US Department of Homeland Security. http://www.history.com/topics/slavery.

Horn, James. 1996. "Leaving England: The Social Background of Indentured Servants in the Seventeenth Century." Jamestown Interpretive Essays. *Virtual Jamestown,* http://www.virtualjamestown.org/essays/horn_essay.html

Kandel, William A. 2011. *The US Foreign-Born Population: Trends and Selected*

Characteristics, R41592. Washington, D.C.: Congressional Research Service.

Koplow, David. 2003. *Smallpox: The Fight to Eradicate a Global Scourge.* Berkeley: University of California Press.

Keesler, M. Paul. 2004. "Iroquois." *In Mohawk: Discovering the Valley of the Crystals,* http://www.mpaulkeeslerbooks.com/Chap5Iroquois. html#Dutch Children.

Kennedy, Edward M. 1981. "Refugee Act of 1980." *International Migration Review* 15 (1):141-156.

Kerwin, Donald. 2010. "More than IRCA: U.S. Legalization Programs and the Current Policy Debate." *MPI Policy Brief.* Washington, D.C.: Migration Policy Institute.

Klein, Herbert S. 2004. *A Population History of the United States.* Cambridge: Cambridge University Press.

Livi Bacci, Massimo. 2008. *Conquest: The Destruction of the American Indios.* New York: Wiley.

Lord, Lewis. 1997. "How Many People Were Here Before Columbus?" *US News & World Report,* August 10.

Lowell, Waverly B. 1996. *Chinese Immigration and Chinese in the United States.* Paper 99. Washington, D.C.: United States National Archives. http://www.archives.gov/research/chinese-americans/guide.html.

Mancke, Elizabeth and Carole Shammas. 2005. *The Creation of the British Atlantic World.* Baltimore, MD: Johns Hopkins University Press.

Martin, Daniel C. and James E. Yankay. 2012. *Refugees and Asylees: 2011, Annual Flow Report.* Office of Immigration Statistics Policy Directorate. Washington, D.C.: Department of Homeland Security. http://www.dhs.gov/xlibrary/assets/statistics/publications/ois_rfa_fr_2011.pdf.

Migration Policy Institute. 2013. *Detailed Review of the 2013 Senate Legislation and Side-by-Side Comparison with 2006, 2007 Senate Bills.* Issue brief No. 4. Washington D.C.: Migration Policy Institute. http://www.migrationpolicy.org/pubs/CIRbrief-2013SenateBill-

Side-by-Side.pdf.

Miller, Randall M. and John D. Smith. eds. 1988. *Dictionary of Afro-American Slavery.* Westport, CT: Greenwood Press.

Monger, Randall and James Yankay. 2013. *US Legal Permanent Residents: 2012 Annual Flow Report.* Office of Immigration Statistics Policy Directorate. Washington, D.C.: Department of Homeland Security. http://www.dhs.gov/sites/default/files/publications/ois_lpr_fr_2012_2.pdf

Motel, Seth and Eileen Patten. 2013. "Statistical Portrait of the Foreign-Born Population in the United States, 2011." Pew ResearchHispanic Center, 29 January. http://www.pewhispanic.org/2013/01/29/statistical-portrait-of-the-foreign-born-population-in-the-united-states-2011/

Navarro, Armando. 2005. *Mexicano Political Experience in Occupied Aztlan: Struggles and Changes.* Walnut Creek, CA: Alta Mira Press.

Passel, Jeffrey and D'Vera Cohn. 2012. "Unauthorized Immigrants: 11.1 Million in 2011." Pew Research Hispanic Center, December. http://www.pewhispanic.org/2012/12/06/unauthorized-immigrants-11-1-million-in-2011/

Pfaelzer, Jean. 2007. *Driven Out: The Forgotten War Against Chinese Americans.* New York: Random House.

Philbrick, Nathaniel. 2006. *Mayflower: A Story of Courage, Community, and War.* New York: Viking Press.

Rosenbaum, Alan S., ed. 2001. *Is the Holocaust Unique: Perspectives on Comparative Genocide.* Boulder, CO: Westview Press.

Smith, Daniel Scott. 1972. "The Demographic History of Colonial New England," *Journal of Economic History* 32(1): 165-183.

Spring, Joel. 2001. *Globalization and Educational Rights: An Intercivilizational Analysis.* Lawrence Erlbaum Associates, Inc, Mahwah, NJ.

Steckel, R. H. 2000. "The African American Population of the United States, 1790-1920." *In A Population History of North America,* edited by Michael Haines and Richard Steckel. Cambridge: Cambridge

University Press.

Tallant, Harold D. 1998. "The Columbian Biological Exchange." Last updated December 3, 1998.
http://spider.georgetowncollege.edu/htallant/courses/his111/columb.htm

Taylor, Alan. 2002. *American Colonies: Volume I.* London: Penguin Books.

Taylor, Quintard. 2013. "United States History: Timeline 1700-1800." *University of Washington Department of History,*
http://faculty.washington.edu/qtaylor/a_us_history/1700_1800_timeline.htm

Thernstrom, Stephan. 1980. *Harvard Guide to American Ethnic Groups.* Cambridge, MA: Belknap Press of Harvard University.

United Nations. 2000. *Replacement Migration: Is it a Solution to Declining and Ageing Populations?* Department of Social and Economic Affairs Population Division ST/ESA/SER.A/206. New York: United Nations.

———. 2013. *World Population Prospects: The 2012 Revision.* Department of Social and Economic Affairs Population Division ESA/P/WP.227. New York: United Nations.

United States Census Bureau. 1909. *A Century of Population Growth from the First Census of the United States to the Twelfth, 1790-1900.* Washington D.C.: United States Census Bureau.

———. 1949. *A Historical Statistics of the United States, 1789-1945: A Supplement to the Statistical Abstract of the United States.* Washington, D.C.: United States Census Bureau.
http://www2.census.gov/prod2/statcomp/documents/HistoricalStatisticsoftheUnitedStates1789-1945.pdf.

———. 1975. *A Statistical Abstract Supplement, Historical Statistics of the US Colonial Times to 1970.* Washington, D.C.: United States Census Bureau.
http://www2.census.gov/prod2/statcomp/documents/CT1970p2-01.pdf.

———.1976. *Estimated Population of American Colonies 1620 to 1780.* Series Z-19. Washington, D.C.: United States Census Bureau.

————. 2006. *Historical Statistics of the United States: Colonial Times to 1970.* Boston, MA: Cambridge University Press. http://www.census.gov/prod/www/abs/statab.html.

————.2010. "Foreign Born Population as Percent of State Population, 2010." http://www.census.gov/newsroom/pdf/cspan_fb_slides.pdf

————.2011. *Current Population Survey, Annual Social and Economic Supplement, 2011.* Washington, D.C.: United States Census Bureau.

————. 2012a. "Projections of the Population and Components of Change for the United States: 2015-2060. NP2012-T1." December. Washington, D.C.: United States Census Bureau, Population Division.

————. 2012b. *The Foreign-Born Population in the United States.* American Community Survey. ACS-19. May. Washington, D.C.: United States Census Bureau.

United States Department of Homeland Security. *1985 Statistical Yearbook of the Immigration and Naturalization Service.* Washington, D.C.: United States Department of Homeland Security.

————. 2012. *Yearbook of Immigration Statistics.* Washington, D.C.: United States Department of Homeland Security.

United States Senate. 1965. "Subcommittee on Immigration and Naturalization of the Committee on the Judiciary." Washington, D.C., Feb. 10.

Walsh, Lawrence. S. 2000. "The African American Population of the Colonial United States." *In A Population History of the North America.* Boston, MA: Cambridge University Press.

Warren, Robert and John Robert Warren. 2013 "Unauthorized Immigration to the United States: Annual Estimates and Components of Change, by State, 1990 to 2010." *International Migration Review* 47(2): 296-329.

Washington Times. 2005. "Immigration surge called 'highest ever." December 12.

Weisberger, Bernard A. 1994. "A Nation of Immigrants." *American Heritage*

Magazine. February/March, 45(1).

Wilson, Donna M and Herbert C. Northcott. 2008. *Dying and Death in Canada.* Toronto: University of Toronto Press.

Zolberg, Zloberg, Aristide. 2006. *A Nation by Design: Immigration Policy in the Fashioning of America.* New York: Russell Sage Foundation.

CHAPTER II

The Evolution of the United States Immigration Laws

Charles Wheeler

Introduction

U.S. immigration laws tend to reflect the mood of the country at the time they are passed. The overriding concerns have usually been financial and linked to the state of the economy. It is easy to understand why the United States looked for ways to streamline the process of importing laborers during periods of financial boom, for example, or has sought ways to restrict their entry or facilitate their deportation during hard times. However, economic factors alone cannot explain laws that excluded Chinese nationals for decades, imposed quotas that virtually barred southern and eastern Europeans, or allowed for the entry of those fleeing political persecution from certain countries but not others. Nor can they explain why the United States has admitted more persons for humanitarian reasons than any other country in the world. To comprehend the reasons for those laws and policies, one must dig deeper into the American psyche and beyond the lines from the Emma Lazarus poem proclaiming the United States to be a beacon to the world's tired, poor and huddled masses. U.S. immigration laws reflect the nation's history and political movements— its diverse values, competing visions of nationality and membership, and the swinging pendulum of efforts to restrict and liberalize admission policies. They also reflect the human condition, with all its admirable and shameful qualities.

Passage of immigration legislation has often been a long process involving debates, hearings, reports, secret negotiations, amendments, compromises, and even presidential vetoes. Most immigration laws have required years of incubation. Only a small fraction of the bills introduced were ever reported out of committees. And the laws that have emerged have been a mix of cautious first steps to address long-standing challenges and overreactions to perceived threats.

After laws are passed, the burden shifts to the designated federal agency to interpret and implement them, through orders, cables, memos, or formal regulations. The effectiveness of laws depends in large part on the detailed interpretations provided by the administrative agency. In addition, enforcement of laws is dependent on Congress's appropriating adequate funding. While immigration laws tend to be written with a greater degree of specificity than other laws, the implementing agencies have always been granted latitude in how and when to apply them. To re-state a common principle: administration is often as important as legislation. Administrative and appellate courts have also played a significant role in interpreting U.S. immigration law.

State laws and court decisions are also playing an increasingly important role in shaping public attitudes and enforcement actions. For example, some states have expressed their frustration with the federal government's lack of progress in controlling illegal immigration or preventing unauthorized immigrants from obtaining employment, and they have attempted to "fill the gap" by enacting their own laws. The most notorious was a law passed by Arizona in 2007 requiring all businesses to use the federal electronic worker verification system (E-Verify), followed by a sweeping 2010 law making immigration enforcement the responsibility of every state and local official and agency in Arizona.[1] The following year a number of states passed "copycat" measures, such as Alabama that made it a crime to be unauthorized, required schools to check the immigration status of its students, and complicated the ability of the unauthorized to work, rent housing, and enter into contracts.[2]

Lawsuits successfully challenged most of these state laws. In June 2012, the U.S. Supreme Court ruled that two of the three challenged provisions of Arizona's SB 1070 were unconstitutional.[3] The one provision the Court let stand allows Arizona law enforcement to verify the immigration status of any individual they lawfully stop and have a "reasonable suspicion" to believe is unauthorized. Recent trends are swinging in the other direction: some states have passed pro-immigrant legislation. Since 2011, eight states, Washington, D.C. and Puerto Rico have passed bills to extend driving privileges to all residents regardless of immigration status and seven states have passed tuition equity laws permitting unauthorized youth to pay in-state tuition.

Executive power to exercise discretion in the enforcement of immigration laws dates back to the first federal statutes and to the inherent authority of law enforcement agencies to determine how best to use their limited resources. The delegated agencies have been able to apply case-by-case leniency, as reflected in the following powers: humanitarian parole; the setting of bonds; the authority to suspend or cancel deportation or waive grounds of inadmissibility based on evidence of hardship; the exercise of prosecutorial discretion on whether to commence removal proceedings; the granting of "deferred action" status to the sick or elderly; release from detention under "orders of supervision;" and waiving non-immigrant visa requirements for citizens from countries with a

---

1 Support our Law Enforcement and Safe Neighborhoods Act, SB 1070.
2 Alabama Taxpayer and Citizen Protection Act, HB 56.
3 *Arizona v. United States*, 567 U.S. (2012).

history of low visa fraud.

What is also clear from a study of these laws is how imperfect and even unsuccessful some of them were at addressing the problem at hand. This realization would lead Congress to pass subsequent laws that provided even greater detail and prescriptions, which were just as often circumvented or unenforced. This is not to imply that our immigration laws did not profoundly shape the national origin make-up of the United States during the last two hundred years. But it is worth remembering that the wretched, the homeless, and the huddled masses yearning to breathe free—and to a larger extent the strong, the enterprising, and the industrious—were also able to find ways around those laws and enter or remain here notwithstanding them.

Even a casual look back at the history of U.S. immigration laws reveals certain patterns and repeated themes, many of which will become apparent in this chapter. For example, the United States electorate has always harbored conflicting opinions about the benefits of immigration: almost universal gratitude for the hard work and accomplishments of prior generations of immigrants coupled with suspicion and doubt about the need for current or future immigrants. From the days of the earliest settlements, members of the populace have criticized the latest wave of immigrants for their alleged inability to assimilate, low intelligence, propensity for crime, or lack of education, even though within a generation these workers or their offspring have taken their place among the nation's middle class.

The United States has also shown an ambivalence concerning the need to vigorously enforce its borders against illegal immigration. It was not until the mid-1950s that guarding the U.S.-Mexican border began to be taken seriously. And Congress has only recently authorized enough agents and technology to effectively control the flow. This historic tolerance of a certain level of illegal immigration is due at least in part to an acceptance that the United States is dependent on low-skilled workers to fill certain jobs—for example in farm labor, meat packing, or janitorial work—that U.S. native workers do not want, at least at current wage levels. It also reflects the reality that immigration restrictions for at least the last fifty years have not allowed for the admission of enough lawful temporary workers to meet labor needs.

Other trends have also emerged. Periods of high immigration have tended to be followed by anti-immigrant backlash, while periods of low immigration resulting from restrictionist legislation or economic downturn have often been followed by spikes in immigration levels. A high profile criminal act by a non-citizen is usually followed by scapegoating and "get tough" legislative efforts. Punitive legislation that eliminated benefits or imposed harsh burdens is often amended in subsequent years by softening the prescriptions until Congress "gets it right." This can be seen, for example, in various laws passed in 1986 that were later relaxed four years later.

Immigration flows are still largely driven by economic conditions in the United States and in the sending countries, but they have also been affected by changes in enforcement patterns. Tighter enforcement historically has been coupled with the need to create more secure identity and travel documents, including passports, and more recently those evidencing employment eligibility. This has resulted in the concomitant rise of a black market in counterfeit documents.

The arguments for and against immigration do not always follow traditional political lines, and they often cut across what are typically viewed as conservative and liberal philosophies. Those who favor tighter controls may do so for disparate reasons: cultural, environmental/ecological, xenophobic, racist, or labor-protection. Those who favor increased immigration may be driven by religious, humanitarian, libertarian, or purely capitalistic motivations. Immigration has been made into a political "wedge" issue in countless elections, and has been used to appeal to groups from all sides of the political spectrum—from the self-proclaimed patriots, to nativists, to civil libertarians, to advocates from emerging ethnic or religious bases. One need only open a newspaper or turn on a radio to experience the current discussion over the problems with the immigration system and what action Congress should take to address it, which is not dissimilar in substance or style from those conducted throughout U.S. history. The debate over immigration policy appears to be one of the few constant and reliable features of the U.S. political fabric.

1. The First Immigration Laws: The Colonies and the States

It may come as a surprise to learn that U.S. immigration laws had their origin in those enacted by the colonies, and subsequently by the states. Many of the same issues faced by the federal government in the late nineteenth century when it started asserting control—the exclusion of those deemed undesirable, the deportation of those who committed crimes or engaged in prohibited activity, and the enforcement of borders—had been experienced by the colonies almost two hundred years earlier.

The colonists actively promoted immigration, but they also faced questions about how to welcome the latest wave of newcomers, and their attitudes and reactions were not always positive. Some of the first laws prohibited the settling of those from certain religious faiths, in an effort to maintain homogeneity. Other laws prohibited admission of the sick, the infirm, and the indigent, unless a bond could be posted. Particular attention and legislation concerned those who might become a public charge. The burden of ensuring the admission of passengers was placed on the ship commander, who in turn passed along this risk to the passengers in the form of higher fares.

During this period, the British government engaged in the practice of shipping criminals to the colonies, which resulted in colonial laws to thwart "penal transportation." Several colonies, particularly those in the south and mid-Atlantic, passed legislation holding the transporter responsible for any felon who was seeking admission, which required the posting of a surety that would be forfeited if the alien committed further crimes. Other laws simply excluded those who had committed certain offenses.

For example, one law passed by the Delaware Colony in 1740 is titled, "An Act Imposing a Duty on Persons Convicted of Heinous Crimes and to Prevent Poor and Impotent Persons being Imported." It was typical of these laws at that time, and singled out persons who were likely to become a public charge or who had engaged in criminal activity. The colonies introduced the concept of grounds of inadmissibility, which is an important part of U.S. immigration law today. This particular law addressed those who were aged, disabled, low income, or who had a mental disorder. It also singled out those who had committed certain offenses, which today would be classified as "crimes involving moral turpitude." The Delaware Colony law required the ship captain both to pay a fine and post a bond, which would be released after a period of time only if the immigrant demonstrated good behavior.

Many early citizens expressed negative views about admitting more immigrants. For example, William Shaw, John Adams' nephew, wrote on May 20, 1798, shortly before he was made the President's private secretary: "I believe the grand cause of all our present difficulties may be traced to this source—too many hordes of Foreigners to America... Let us no longer pray that America may become an asylum to all nations, but let us encourage our own men and cultivate our simple manners" (Rosenfeld 1996, 129).

It was during this era that the regulation of immigrants, the recording of identifying information, and the maintenance of these records, first began. Head taxes were imposed, both to fund this record-keeping, but also to act as a financial restraint on further immigration. State action up through the mid-1800s continued much of this compulsory reporting, inspection of alien passengers, and taxation of arrivals. Policing of land and sea borders became a concern, due to efforts by ship captains to circumvent these laws. In many ways, the immigration issues faced in the 1700s do not look significantly different from those of today.

2. Federal Action: The First Hundred Years

When the United States was formally founded it was generally taken for granted that immigration was vital to the country's future prosperity: more settlers were needed to populate a vast empty land and tap its wealth. The Declaration of Independence faulted King George III for his "endeavor[ing] to prevent the population of these States; for that purpose obstructing the Laws for Naturalization of Foreigners; refusing to pass others to encourage their migrations hither."[4]

Statements from the Founding Fathers generally lauded the benefits of immigrants and the need for more workers. George Washington addressed head-on the question of whether immigrants should be encouraged to come and countered the perception that they tend to "retain the Language, habits and principles (good or bad) which they bring with them. Whereas by an intermixture with our people, they, or their descendants, get assimilated to our customs, measures and laws: in a word, soon become one people."[5]

Benjamin Franklin was one of the most outspoken: "Strangers are welcome because there is room enough for them all, and therefore the old Inhabitants are not jealous of them; the Laws protect them sufficiently so that they have no need of the Patronage of great Men; and every one will enjoy securely the Profits of his Industry."[6] Yet even he was conflicted, for twenty years earlier he had argued against the immigration of more Germans, describing them as "the most stupid of their nation." And he went on to conclude: "Unless the stream of their importation can be turned from this to other colonies…they will soon so outnumber us, that all the advantages we have will not in My Opinion be able to preserve our language, and even

---

4 U.S. Declaration of Independence, July 4, 1776.
5 George Washington, letter to John Adams, 1794.
6 Benjamin Franklin, "Those Who Would Remove to America," 1784.

our Government will be precarious."[7]   It would appear from those remarks that anti-immigrant sentiment and prejudice is older than America itself, and this fear that immigrants from certain countries would dilute the "American" heritage and traditions has pervaded its immigration policies.

Given that immigrants were such an essential—if somewhat controversial—part of the framework of the United States when it was founded, it is curious that while the U.S. Constitution gave Congress the power to regulate naturalization, it was silent on its power to regulate immigration.[8] One answer might be that it was so self-evident as to not require specific language. But another could be the assumption that states should be allowed to exercise power in this area, since at that time they controlled entrance through their borders of both citizens and foreigners. Only later would the government's power "to regulate Commerce with foreign Nations and among the several states" be invoked to authorize its exclusive powers over immigration.[9]

The first federal law affecting immigration was passed in 1790 when Congress restricted U.S. citizenship to "free white persons...of good moral character."[10] This law was intended to exclude indentured servants and slaves from acquiring citizenship.   Non-citizens could apply for "naturalization" after a two-year waiting period, which was soon extended to five years. But in 1798, this period was extended to fourteen years and required the filing of a "declaration of intent" to naturalize five years prior to eligibility.[11] This law was motivated by a fear that too many Irish and French immigrants would tip the political balance at that time. But four years later, after a change in presidential and congressional leadership, the five-year residency requirement was restored and the declaration of intent reduced to three years.[12]

To illustrate the pervasive influence of racial prejudices throughout U.S. immigration laws, naturalization remained restricted to "white persons" until 1870, when it was finally opened up to blacks after the Civil War.[13] But it took until 1940 for "races indigenous to the Western hemisphere," which

7 Kenneth C. Davis, "The Founding Immigrants," *New York Times*, July 3, 2007.
8 Art. 1, sec. 8, clause 4 ("Congress shall have the Power... to establish a uniform Rule of Naturalization.").
9 Art. 1, sec. 8, clause 3.
10 Naturalization Act of 1790, 1 Stat. 103.
11 Act of June 18, 1798, 1 Stat 566.
12 Act of April 14, 1802, 2 Stat 153.
13 Act of July 14, 1870, 16 Stat 254.

predominantly affected Mexicans, to be eligible to naturalize.[14] This was followed soon by legislation permitting Chinese—who had been specifically classified as non-white by the Supreme Court [15]—to naturalize. It was not until 1952 when all racial bars to naturalization were finally removed.[16]

In 1798, the United States passed the infamous Alien and Sedition Acts that granted the President almost unlimited power to remove without a hearing "all such aliens as he shall judge dangerous to the peace and safety of the United States."[17] The motivating factor at that time was a perceived threat from enemy nations and foreign influences in the wake of the French Revolution. The laws were allowed to expire after two years due to their unpopularity. However, they created a significant precedent, namely the power of the federal government to detain and deport noncitizens when it deemed it necessary. James Madison lambasted the law as "a monster that must forever disgrace its parents."[18] The Supreme Court criticized the law for banishing non-citizens from "a country where he may have formed the most tender connections."[19]

The second significant precedent occurred in 1819 when Congress passed legislation dealing with the regulation of passenger ships. While the provisions were intended mostly to protect the safety and welfare of those onboard trans-Atlantic vessels, the law went further and required ship captains to maintain and turn over passenger manifests.[20] The federal government's statistical record-keeping on immigration to the United States, as well as its effort to assert some control over who entered the country, date from this early law.

Immigration to the United States flourished during the 1800s due to the demand for labor and the supply of jobs in ever-increasing industries, such as agriculture, construction, railroads, and manufacturing. The mid-nineteenth century discovery of gold in California led to mass internal migration, but also created the demand for more foreign workers, particularly those from China. The accepted attitude during the early to mid-1880s was that immigrants were essential to this economic growth, as well as a general belief that America should welcome those seeking a better life. The *Homestead Act of 1862*

---

14 Act of October 14, 1940, 54 Stat. 1137.
15 *Fong Yue Ting v. United States,* 149 U.S. 698 (1893).
16 Act of March 20, 1952, 66 Stat. 163.
17 Alien Act of June 25, 1798, 1 Stat. 570.
18 James Madison, Letter to Tomas Jefferson, 1798.
19 *Fong Yue Ting,* 149 U.S. at 743.
20 Act of March 2, 1819, 3 Stat. 488.

encouraged non-citizens to settle the Wild West, and allowed them to own land provided they had filed a declaration of intent to naturalize (Motomura 2006).[21] The country was still untamed at that time, although by the end of the century the frontier was closing and the United States was shifting from agrarian to urban and becoming more industrialized. With that shift came a change in attitudes and rising opposition to both the size of the flow and the source of the immigrants.

Tensions rose on both coasts during that time as new national origin and religious groups started moving into communities that had been relatively homogeneous. Public sentiment turned anti-immigrant and backlashes against Chinese on the west coast and Irish Catholics on the east coast became more pronounced. Political groups that were openly nativist, such as the American Republican Party, the Order of United Americans, and the Know Nothing Party, formed in an effort to push restrictive immigration legislation and keep out "undesirables." The Know Nothing Party, which started out as a "secret" party, championed native-born Protestants and was particularly opposed to Catholics and recent immigrants. Their anti-immigrant rhetoric has been compared to that of some current politicians fighting immigration reform.[22]

But Congress resisted these anti-alien pressures for two principal reasons. First, they reflected the generally pro-immigrant attitudes of the country at that time. After the Civil War, in which a substantial percentage of the soldiers were foreign-born, anti-immigrant sentiments were replaced by more immigrant integration. Second, Congress was wary of asserting too much control over immigration since the question of whether such powers still remained in the states' domain had not yet been resolved. While it was clear that issues touching on naturalization required a uniform national system, the states still believed that they retained powers over the regulation of immigrants entering or remaining within their borders.

At the end of the Civil War, Congress passed the first law stating that all children born on U.S. soil would be conferred U.S. citizenship, regardless of their parents' citizenship status, race, or place of birth.[23] Two years later birthright citizenship was guaranteed by the U.S. Constitution through the

---

21 The Homestead Act, 12 Stat. 392.
22 Craig Shirley, "How the GOP Lost Its Way," *Washington Post*, April 22, 2006, at. A21; "The Immigration Deal," *New York Times,* May 20, 2007.
23 The Civil Rights Act of 1866, 14 Stat. 27.

"citizenship clause" of the Fourteenth Amendment.[24]   In 1898, the Court affirmed that birthright citizenship extended to children born on U.S. soil to resident non-citizen parents.[25]

The principle which confers citizenship based on the person's place of birth, regardless of the status of the child's parents, is referred to as jus soli. This contrasts with *jus sanguinis*, which bases citizenship on descent and the citizenship of the parent(s). Europe followed the latter principle, while the United States adopted both forms of acquiring citizenship—through either birth in the United States or birth abroad to one or both U.S. citizen parents.

It was not until 1875 that Congress introduced the concept of inadmissibility by passing a law prohibiting the admission of women "imported for the purposes of prostitution."[26] Another section excluded felons, other than those convicted of purely political offenses. The same law addressed the growing anti-Chinese feelings by prohibiting the importation of Oriental persons entering "without their free and voluntary consent." This provision tried to cut off "coolie labor"; e.g. by Chinese nationals imported under contracts requiring them to work for a designated employer at a specified wage and for a period necessary to pay off the costs of their passage. Californians in particular viewed such arrangements as too close to indentured servitude, in addition to believing that Chinese workers undercut wages and competed unfairly with local workers.

The 1875 law is seen by many as the beginning of direct federal regulation of immigration. Throughout the first half of the 1800s, the courts had upheld the power of the states to regulate immigration as long as their laws did not conflict with the federal government's power to regulate commerce or foreign affairs. For example, in 1837 the U.S. Supreme Court held that a state law requiring the maintenance of ship manifests was constitutional.[27] But by the middle of the century, courts started striking down state legislation affecting immigration under the principle that the Constitution vested such powers exclusively with the federal government. In the most famous cluster of cases, known as the Passenger Cases, the Supreme Court held that a state's imposition of a head tax and the posting of bonds violated the federal government's

---

24 U.S. Const. Amend. XIV, § 1.
25 *U.S. v. Wong Kim Ark*, 169 US 649 (1898).
26 Immigration Act of March 3, 1875, 18 Stat. 477.
27 *City of New York v. Miln*, 36 U.S. 102 (1837).

commerce power.[28] This principle was affirmed in 1876 by the Supreme Court in two decisions striking down similar California and New York laws as infringing on the federal power to regulate commerce with foreign nations.[29] With the states' rights claim now put to rest, Congress started moving in to fill this void and to address the needs and demands of those various states and the nation as a whole.

Beginning in 1875 and covering a fifty-year period, Congress became active in constructing various exclusion and deportation statutes. As late as 1882, immigration regulation was still split between the federal and state governments, with federal immigration authority vested in the Secretary of the Treasury and day-to-day administration handled by the states. But that year Congress expanded the grounds of exclusion to prohibit the admission of those found to be "idiots, lunatics, convicts, and persons likely to become public charges."[30] Those same exclusions exist today and comprise some of the more common ways of denying entry to immigrant visa applicants. The only modern changes have been their re-wording, expansion, and segregation into "health-related," "criminal," and "public charge" grounds of inadmissibility.[31]

Another law, passed six years later, introduced the concept of "temporary" status, where a non-citizen was allowed admission in order to work, but could be deported within one year of entry.[32] Congress did not want to stop immigration during that era, but it did want to assert some controls and restrictions so that new immigrants would be less likely to break laws or engage in labor organizing.

Economic factors and outright racism at both the state and federal levels began to drive immigration laws and policies in the latter part of the nineteenth century. The clearest example was the public antagonism directed at Chinese laborers, which resulted in various state discriminatory laws and eventually the *Chinese Exclusion Act of 1882*.[33] That federal law imposed a country-specific bar to the admission of most Chinese and a ban on their ability to naturalize. It also represented the first time Congress had passed a deportation statute,

---

28 *Smith v. Turner*, 48 U.S. 283 (1849).
29 *Chy Lung v. Freeman*, 92 U.S. 275 (1876); *Henderson v. Mayor of City of New York*, 92 U.S. 259 (1876).
30 Act of August 3, 1882, 22 Stat. 214.
31 Immigration and Nationality Act (INA) §§ 212(a) (1), (a) (2), and (a) (4).
32 Act of Oct. 19, 1888, 25 Stat. 566.
33 Act of May 6, 1882, 22 Stat. 58.

which targeted "any Chinese person found unlawfully within the United States."[34] The ban on their admission and naturalization was written to expire after ten years, but it was renewed in ten-year increments until 1904, at which point it was extended indefinitely.[35] The Chinese exclusion laws were relaxed in 1930 and finally repealed in 1943,[36] more than sixty years after enactment.

The justification for the ban originated in California, where ninety percent of the Chinese lived, as an effort to protect U.S. workers from perceived unfair competition. But it later spread nationwide based on the following arguments, most of them specious: the Chinese did not enter voluntarily to live in the United States but rather to work as indentured servants; they were willing to work at wages and under conditions that lowered the standards for domestic workers; they failed to assimilate; they were untrustworthy and prone to criminality; they were pagans; and their women engaged freely in prostitution.

The *Chinese Exclusion Act of 1882* marked a turning point in U.S. history because it was the first law that banned a group of immigrants based solely on their race or nationality. It opened the door to allow for race to become a viable basis for excluding persons. Politicians used this issue to stereotype, stir up ethnic hatred, and appeal to working class voters. One Congressman described the "Chinaman" as "loathsome…revolting…a monstrosity…[who] lives in herds and sleeps like a pack of dogs in kennels."[37] Senator James Blaine, who is credited for leading the political attack on Chinese workers and for the ultimate passage of the federal law, used even more outrageous and defamatory language. Unfortunately, it proved to be an effective political strategy, forcing many moderates and liberals to either join the growing restrictionist tide or at least remain silent. This tactic of using immigration, unauthorized immigrants, or a particular nationality group to appeal to an influential block of voters would play out repeatedly in succeeding political campaigns.

The Supreme Court also weighed in at this time to uphold the retroactive application of a federal law that precluded even returning Chinese residents from reentry. In rejecting the due process argument of the excluded Chinese national and upholding Congress's and the federal government's almost unlimited powers over immigration matters, the Court established what has been termed

---

34 Ibid.
35 Act of April 27, 1904, 33 Stat. 428.
36 Act of December 17, 1943, 57 Stat. 600.
37 Congressional Record, 47th Cong., 1st sess., 2132 (Mar. 21, 1882).

the "plenary power" principle.[38] This principle makes it very difficult for non-citizens residing outside the United States to make constitutional arguments challenging laws or procedures finding them excludable; it similarly hampers non-citizens residing in the United States from challenging deportation grounds as unconstitutional. This was later summed up by the Court when it stated: "Congress regularly makes rules [in the immigration context] that would be unacceptable if applied to citizens."[39]

Anti-immigrant sentiment was also pointed against "new immigrants" coming from Southern and Eastern Europe. Many expressed concern that the country was turning from a melting pot into a dumping ground for other countries' undesirables. The increased numbers of these immigrants brought blatant racist sentiment to the surface, stirred up class conflict, and created dire warnings that the "American" value system was being weakened. Many of the same arguments used against Chinese – their inability to assimilate, low intelligence, propensity for crime – were aimed at this target group, leading to eugenics theories in the early 1900s and an effort to lend scientific credence to racial prejudices.

Congress continued this "get tough" sentiment in 1882 with a law that excluded "any person unable to take care of himself or herself without becoming a public charge,"[40] and in 1891 with a law that targeted for deportation persons who had entered the country illegally,[41] an enforcement concept that did not exist before then. It also established a Commissioner of Immigration within the Treasury Department, a move that symbolized the growing importance of addressing immigration issues in a uniform manner from the federal level.

By now Congress had assumed a more muscular role in the regulation of immigrants. But it was still using a relatively cautious and measured approach. It had rejected efforts to impose stiff head taxes, English literacy tests, restrictions on ownership of real estate, and other discriminatory anti-alien measures. These proposals would continue to surface after the turn of the century when the country shifted from mild regulation to more severe bars and annual quotas.

---

38 *Chinese Exclusion Case,* 130 U.S. 581, 606 (1898) ([If Congress] considers the presence of foreigners of a different race in this country, who will not assimilate with us, to be dangerous to its peace and security...its determination is conclusive upon the judiciary.").

39 *Mathews v. Diaz,* 426 U.S. 67 (1976).

40 Act of August 3, 1882, 22 Stat. 214.

41 Act of March 3, 1891, 26 Stat. 1084.

3. Immigration Laws 1900-1950

The first half of the 1900s witnessed a progressive tightening of alien restrictions and efforts to close open land borders. In 1903 Congress passed a lengthy bill containing thirty-nine sections that added more grounds of inadmissibility, including bans on epileptics, those seeking to procure prostitutes, the insane, and persons suffering from a mental or physical disorder that might prevent their gainful employment.[42] It tightened ship manifest requirements, doubled the head tax to two dollars, and allowed for the deportation of any alien who became a public charge within two years of admission. Four years later, President Roosevelt signed legislation that doubled the head tax again, lengthened the list of excludable aliens, and included the manifesting of departing—not just arriving—aliens.[43]

Laws passed in the first half of the twentieth century continued anti-Chinese attitudes, and in certain ways magnified them to encompass immigrants coming from other parts of the world, specifically eastern and southern Europe. A law passed in 1917—after 25 years of failed attempts and four presidential vetoes—finally added the literacy test intended to hinder the immigration of non-English speaking persons.[44] The literacy test resulted in a sharp decline in legal immigration from Mexico and other Latin American countries, though it was applied unevenly.

The 1917 law also created an "Asiatic Barred Zone" that excluded those from South Asia—a large swath stretching from Arabia to Indo-China and the Pacific Islands. Japanese workers had been exempted from the bars affecting the Chinese because they were valued for their contribution to the agricultural industry in northern California. But this informal agreement with the Japanese government soon expired and they too were excluded.

Immigration laws had now shifted from protecting against targeted issues to reflecting openly racist and ethnocentric biases. But the law that most demonstrated this prejudice—albeit in a more disguised manner—was the Quota Act enacted in 1924, which attempted to freeze the national origin make-up of the country as it existed at that time.[45] It set annual limits on the number of aliens admitted from a specific country to three percent of

---

42 Act of March 3, 1903, 32 Stat. 1213.
43 Immigration Act of February 20, 1907, 34 Stat. 898.
44 Act of Feb. 5, 1917, 39 Stat. 874.
45 Act of May 26, 1924, 43 Stat. 153.

the country's representation in the United States as of 1910. Exempted from the quota were citizens from Western Hemisphere countries, which included Canada, Mexico, the Caribbean, and Central and South America. Three years later, Congress strengthened the quota restrictions even further by setting the cap at two percent of the 1890 base population.[46] Beginning in 1929, the annual quota was set at 150,000 immigrants, allocated based on the national origin distribution of the population in 1920.[47]

The intent of the quotas was to encourage immigration from certain favored nations while lowering it from disfavored ones. The result was that persons from central, northern, and western European countries were allowed to immigrate in much larger numbers than their counterparts from other parts of the continent or the world. Asians continued to be barred under the Quota Act, because they were "ineligible to citizenship," which was part of the standard for admission. This system was finally abolished in 1965. But by then the national origin make-up of the country had been weighted heavily in favor of persons from Great Britain, France, Germany, and Scandinavian countries.

The other effect of this quota system was to slow immigration in the decades following its enactment. For example, 14.5 million persons immigrated during the twenty-year period from 1901-1920, while less than one million immigrated during the ten-year period from 1931-1940 (DHS 2013, Table 1). The rules restricting the flow of immigrants, as well as an expansion in the grounds of deportable offenses, came into full play during the Great Depression. During that period there were years when more persons emigrated from the United States than immigrated to the United States.

The 1924 law also created an important distinction between those who enter with the intention of residing in the United States permanently (immigrants) and those who enter temporarily to study or visit (non-immigrants).[48] This categorical distinction plays a key role today in determining eligibility for admission to the United States. Immigrants are permitted to remain in the country indefinitely and enjoy many of the same rights and benefits as U.S. citizens. The major distinction is that U.S. citizens enjoy the ability to vote, protection from deportation, and eligibility for a full range of public benefits and employment options. In contrast, non-immigrants are only allowed to enter for a designated period and a specified purpose, and must demonstrate

46 Ibid.
47 Act of March 4, 1929, 45 Stat 1551.
48 Act of May 19, 1921, 42 Stat 5.

their intention to resume residency in their home country.

The Chinese Exclusion Act and the quota system created the need to capture the identity and national origin of applicants for admission (Robertson 2010, 171-74). Thus began the passage of additional laws requiring the issuance of passports and identity documents, which led to the requirement that photographs be included on these documents and that they be certified by an issuing agency. Persons seeking entry into the United States needed first to obtain a visa from a U.S. consulate abroad. This requirement, in turn, led to the manufacturing and selling of fraudulent identity documents and visas, a practice that until recent years—which have seen increasingly counterfeit-proof documents —largely kept pace with tightening security measures.

Another reason for excluding and deporting certain immigrants also emerged at that time: political ideology or affiliation. The first law that introduced this ban was enacted in 1903 and it barred "anarchists or persons who believed in or advocated the overthrow by force or violence of the Government of the United States or all government."[49] In 1917, those who engaged in "subversive activities" were similarly barred. One year later, in reaction to the Russian Revolution and the "Red Scare," Congress added "anarchists" to those who were deportable.[50] This was done specifically to quell labor organizing efforts that had become popular and successful. Later, during the McCarthy era of the 1950s, Congress added those who were "politically dangerous" to the list of excludable persons.[51] The ban on those who were "voluntary" members of the Communist Party remained as part of the law even after the Cold War had ended. Iranians were targeted after the hostage seizure at the U.S. Embassy in 1979. The present day equivalent would be the exclusion of members or supporters of a "foreign terrorist organization."[52]

During the period from 1915 to 1920, thousands of persons were arrested, detained, and deported for their efforts to organize farmworkers and other laborers. In one notorious round-up in 1917, 1,300 striking mine workers were arrested, loaded onto cattle cars, and transported from Bisbee, Arizona to the Mexican border in what has been viewed as a flagrantly illegal act on the part of state officials. In 1924 Congress added an important ground of

49 Act of March 3, 1903, 32 Stat. 1213.
50 Act of October 16, 1918, 40 Stat. 1012.
51 Internal Security Act of September 23, 1950, 64 Stat. 987.
52 INA § 212(a) (3) (B) (i).

deportability for those who had entered the country illegally at any time, giving it more power to remove striking workers.[53] Economic factors, combined with anti-labor organizing efforts, resulted in massive deportations of Mexicans from the Southwest in the 1930s. The most notorious round-ups occurred two decades later. Under "Operation Wetback," the U.S. Border Patrol forced the return of thousands of unauthorized Mexicans who were working in the Rio Grande Valley and other parts of Texas.

In 1929 Congress added an important avenue for unauthorized persons who had been in the United States for an eight-year period to apply directly for immigrant status.[54] Titled "registry," this benefit had few requirements other than proving residence in the country and demonstrating good moral character. Since 1929, the law has been amended four times to update the qualifying period of unauthorized residence. The last time the registry date was amended was in 1986 when the qualifying date was changed from June 30, 1948 to January 1, 1972. More than 72,000 persons have adjusted status based on the most recent updating (Kerwin 2010, 12).

The *Alien Registration Act of 1940* mandated the fingerprinting of all aliens aged 14 or over who were either present in the country or seeking admission.[55] It also made them deportable for past membership in subversive organizations. In certain ways, this law reflected the shift from viewing immigrants a hundred years earlier as needed workers to the image of them at that time as potential trouble-makers.

This shift was also reflected in the emergence and transfer of power over immigration and enforcement. In 1906, Congress created the Bureau of Immigration, which was later expanded to the Bureau of Immigration and Naturalization. At that time, the federal government began assuming jurisdiction over naturalization applications, which up until then had been adjudicated in a non-uniform way by the various states. The Bureau was originally part of the Treasury Department, but it was relocated to the Department of Commerce and Labor. In 1924 Congress established the Border Patrol within that same department, which was largely a result of the Chinese Exclusion Act and the resulting need to control the border and check for proper identity and entry documents. In 1933, the Immigration and Naturalization Service (INS) was created and was joined with the Border Patrol. In 1940, they were both

53 Act of May 26, 1924, 43 Stat. 153.
54 Act of May 2, 1929, 45 Stat. 1512.
55 Act of June 28, 1940, 54 Stat. 670.

transferred from Commerce and Labor to the Department of Justice, as border and interior enforcement were made more of a priority. After the terrorist attacks of 2011, the agency was re-named and transferred to the Department of Homeland Security (DHS), where it now resides.

The *Bracero* program, which was implemented in 1942, was initially designed as a short-term answer to Southwestern growers' need for farmworkers due to the labor shortage during World War II.[56] It allowed Mexicans to enter and work during the growing months, but then return to their country after the harvest. After the war ended, however, growers were unwilling to give up this cheap source of labor, and the program continued until 1964, at which time it was formally abolished. During the intervening years, millions of Mexicans left their small farms in rural Mexico and traveled to the United States to perform seasonal farm labor, typically returning to their homes in the off-season.

The *Bracero* program created a further co-dependence between Mexico and the United States, and changed prior migration flows, labor practices, and employment options. Among the changes that continue to affect both countries, the program led to the expansion of labor-intensive agribusiness in the United States and the concomitant drying up of certain industries south of the border, in addition to the often long-term separation of families left behind in Mexico. While officially about 400,000 Mexicans entered the United States annually as *Braceros* during that 22-year period, thousands more entered without authorization and had little trouble finding work as manual laborers. The program also led to the development of channels for unauthorized migration and businesses on both sides of the border that facilitate the transportation of eager workers to needy employers.

4. Immigration Acts of 1952 and 1965

In 1952, the United States entered what is considered the modern era of immigration law if for no other reason than Congress repealed all prior legislation and codified the immigration laws at that time into one document: the *Immigration and Nationality Act* (INA) of June 27, 1952.[57] Practitioners today use the INA as one of their principal reference tools, even though after sixty years of annual amendments, revisions, and expansions, it bears only faint

---

56 The *Bracero* program began as an executive agreement between the United States and Mexico and was revised and legalized by Congress in 1943 and in subsequent years. See, e.g., the 1951 legislation at 65 Stat. 119.

57 McCarran-Walter Act of June 27, 1952, 66 Stat. 163.

resemblance to its original text.

The 1952 Act changed the administration of the national quota system to make it appear fairer and more nationality-neutral. It removed overt racial barriers to immigration and naturalization, though it kept the quotas small for those of Asian or Pacific ancestry. It allowed for the non-quota immigration of spouses and children of U.S. citizens, and created "preference" categories for other relatives of U.S. citizens and lawful permanent residents (LPRs). It also added preference categories for skilled workers. All of these changes formed the framework for our current immigration system and the allocation of immigrant visas.

The Act increased the ways that an alien could be denied entry by including the following grounds: dangerous and contagious diseases (e.g., leprosy), multiple criminal offenses with an aggregate sentence of five years or more, narcotic drug addicts, and fraud or misrepresentation. It cracked down on those who entered or attempted to enter the country illegally. In addition, it created more grounds of deportation by broadening the classes of aliens defined as subversive. These classifications exist in whole or in part today.

The 1952 Act also built on post-war legislation to assist hardship cases, which had allowed for the admission of over 300,000 refugees, war orphans, and displaced persons.[58] The Act added fear of political persecution as a basis for the withholding of an alien's deportation. Almost thirty years later, this concept would blossom formally into asylum and refugee law. Before 1980, however, this provision was used principally as a basis for granting protections to those fleeing communist countries, and not to those fleeing oppression in right-wing, dictatorial ones. In 1966, Congress passed the Cuban Adjustment Act, which provided special treatment and eligibility for permanent residency to anyone who successfully escaped from Castro's regime.[59]

Much of these laws and policy decisions were part of Cold War efforts to counter Russia's growing influence and demonstrate a more attractive alternative. The United States wanted to be an example to the world of freedom, liberty, and a sanctuary for the oppressed. The message was clear: choose democracy and capitalism and you will be liberated rather than suffering under the chains of communism and a totalitarian state. But the U.S. admission policy for refugees was not applied evenly. For example, the Cuban

58 Displaced Persons Act of June 25, 1948, 62 Stat 1009.
59 Cuban Adjustment Act of November 2, 1966, 79 Stat. 919.

Adjustment Act stood in stark contrast to the treatment and lack of benefits afforded those fleeing political oppression in Haiti, the Dominican Republic, or Central America, particularly during the turbulent 1970s and 1980s.

But a true turning point in U.S. immigration law occurred in 1965 when Congress overhauled the quota system to officially remove national origin as a basis for excluding persons, most notably those from Asia.[60] This was during the Civil Rights movement, and the removal was equated as repeal of the racial bars that existed in the United States at that time. However, Congress imposed a quota on those from Western Hemisphere countries (120,000 visas per year), which up until then had been free to immigrate outside of any annual limitations. Those from Eastern Hemisphere countries were allowed 170,000 visas, bringing the total worldwide quota to 290,000 immigrant visas per year. Individual countries from the Eastern Hemisphere were subject to a per-country limit of 20,000 visas, while those from the Western Hemisphere were not subject to that restriction. That would come eleven year later, when the per-country limits would be applied worldwide.

The 1965 Act focused on reunifying family members, attracting skilled workers, and protecting those fearing persecution. U.S. citizens were eligible to petition for spouses, children, parents, and siblings. LPRs were eligible to petition for only spouses and unmarried children. Family-based immigration set up two categories: "immediate relatives," who immigrated outside of any worldwide quota; and those in the preference categories, who were subject to the annual quota and potentially long delays until a visa became available.

The employment-based immigration system, which granted visas based on education, experience, and ability, was subject to its own preference categories and quotas. Depending on the category, most applicants first had to apply for a "labor certification" from the Department of Labor. That agency would need to certify that there were an insufficient number of U.S. workers willing, able, qualified, and available for that job, and that employment of the alien for whom certification is sought would not adversely affect the wages and working conditions of U.S. workers similarly employed. After the certification was obtained, they were then eligible to petition for permanent residency when their particular visa category became available.

The 1965 Act further expanded the protections afforded those who feared persecution in their home country by adding race, religion, and political

60 Act of October 3, 1965, 79 Stat. 911.

opinion as a basis for admission. Fifteen years later, when Congress passed the *Refugee Act of 1980,* the standard was expanded to include national origin and membership in a particular social group, and it was applied both to those temporarily residing in a third country (refugees) and those residing in the United States (asylum applicants). A separate division of the INS was later formed to accept and adjudicate asylum claims, while the United Nations High Commission for Refugees was delegated the task of interviewing applicants for refugee status.

5. Immigration Reform and Control Act of 1986

The build-up to the *Immigration Reform and Control Act* (IRCA), which was signed into law on November 6, 1986, began more than a decade earlier with various presidential and congressional efforts to address a number of competing pressures. Anti-immigrant sentiments had been rising, due largely to a post-Vietnam economic recession and the usual nativist sentiments.

Government- and media-driven campaigns painted a picture of large numbers of unauthorized workers crossing a largely unguarded southern border, taking jobs that should have gone to U.S. citizens, and then committing crimes or applying for welfare benefits. These campaigns fueled public perceptions, which contrasted with the numerous studies that concluded the opposite: that unauthorized workers generally took low-paying jobs and did not compete with U.S. workers; they were an overall benefit to the U.S. economy; they were incarcerated at rates below U.S. citizens; and they contributed far more to the federal coffers through their taxes than they received through public benefit programs.

At the same time, civil rights groups mounted an outcry against the raids and mass deportations taking place, and argued in favor of a legalization program for the estimated three to five million unauthorized persons living in the United States at that time.

In 1976, Congress had amended the INA in a number of significant ways. It had replaced the hemispheric ceilings with worldwide and uniform per-country limits on the number of persons who could immigrate.[61] The quotas for Eastern and Western Hemisphere countries became standardized at 20,000 visas each. Children born in the United States of unauthorized parents were no longer able to petition for their parents' lawful immigration status until

---

61 Immigration and Nationality Act of 1978, 92 Stat 907.

they turned 21. Persons who had entered the country legally were allowed to "adjust" their status in the United States, while those who had entered without authorization were still required to leave and obtain an immigrant visa at a U.S. consulate abroad. This important bifurcation between "adjustment" to LPR status (which occurs within the United States) and consular processing (which occurs outside the United States) remains a feature of the U.S. immigration system.

Limiting the number of immigrant visas to 20,000 per year impacted Mexicans more than any other country, since before that time they had been able to immigrate outside of any per-country cap. The result was the creation of long backlogs in the family-based visa categories and an increase in illegal immigration from that country.

To study the push and pull factors causing illegal immigration and make recommendations for a possible comprehensive overhaul of the laws, President Carter appointed a Select Commission on Immigration and Refugee Policy in 1980, which traveled the country holding hearings before releasing a report in June 1981. Among its finding were the following: the need for a law prohibiting employers from knowingly hiring unauthorized workers; a requirement that new hires show documentation verifying their citizenship or lawful immigration status; increased enforcement along the U.S.-Mexico border; a large-scale amnesty for farmworkers and one for those who have been residing in the United States without immigration status since before a certain date; and expansion in the number of family-based visas—especially for Mexican nationals—to address the backlog. Each of those findings would later form the main components of IRCA, though it would take five years of legislative debate and political wrangling to reach an eventual compromise.

IRCA is best remembered for its amnesty programs and for employer sanctions: the yin and yang of immigration reform. The one-time legalization of almost three million unauthorized persons would be countered by increased border enforcement, employment verification requirements, and sanctions against employers who violated them. This was all done in order to weaken the "magnet" that pulled immigrants to the country and to reduce permanently the U.S. unauthorized population. Congress also authorized a fifty percent increase in funding for the Border Patrol.

The two main immigration programs under IRCA were the general amnesty and the farmworker programs. Foreign-born persons who had entered the United States before January 1, 1982 and who were out of status on that date qualified to file for temporary residency. If granted, they were later eligible to file for permanent residency two and a half years later, upon a showing of English language proficiency and knowledge of U.S. civics. Special agricultural workers (SAWs) who had worked a certain number of days in seasonal employment were also eligible to apply. Those who were granted temporary residency automatically converted to permanent residency on one of two dates, depending on how many days they had worked performing seasonal agricultural labor. Approximately 1.6 million persons legalized under the general amnesty law and 1.1 million under the SAW program.

IRCA imposed mandatory employment verification requirements on employers. Every new employee was required to complete a form indicating his or her eligibility to work lawfully in the United States, and submit supporting documentation. The employer's obligation was to examine such documentation for any obvious signs of fraud and to maintain the forms as part of their record-keeping. IRCA failed to prevent the employment of unauthorized workers, who turned to the black market for fraudulent documents. Political pressure from the business community resulted in lax enforcement efforts and deterred Congress from tightening the "loophole." In the end, IRCA did little to take away the magnet of U.S. jobs. Employer sanctions served mainly to spawn a document-fraud industry for those needing paperwork. Anti-immigrant politicians and groups have repeatedly argued that the experience of IRCA should discourage lawmakers from considering legalization measures before an effective enforcement system is in place.

IRCA's failure to curb illegal immigration was due to a variety of reasons, only some of which can be attributed to the law itself. Some policy analysts have argued that the law's legalization provisions did not go far enough. By setting the legalization cut-off date at January 1, 1982, they argue, Congress barred too many people from eligibility and left them without status, paving the way for the subsequent growth of the unauthorized population. Only later, in 1990, did Congress allow the unauthorized spouses and children of those who had legalized to remain in the country in a temporary status.[62] IRCA also failed to address the needs of employers for a temporary workforce that can enter legally on short notice and then depart after the season or work has been

---

62 Immigration Act of 1990, 104 Stat. 4976.

completed.[63]

One day after enacting IRCA, Congress passed the Immigration Marriage Fraud Amendments (IMFA), which imposed restrictions on aliens who obtain permanent residence based on marriage to a U.S. citizen or LPR.[64] The most significant change IMFA made was to create a two-year "conditional residence" status for the alien spouses who immigrate within two years of their marriage to a U.S. citizen.[65] The conditional resident must then take additional steps—including re-establishing the bona fides of the marriage—to remove the conditional status at the end of the two-year period.   It also imposed severe penalties on persons found to have entered into a sham, or fraudulent, marriage.[66] A sham marriage is one where the parties do not intend to establish a life together as spouses but rather to circumvent immigration laws.[67] IMFA's provisions were successful in making it more difficult to immigrate by way of a fraudulent marriage and less attractive to try, but it also served to force conditional residents to remain in abusive relationships. The law originally allowed for a waiver of the conditional status only if the alien spouse could prove that he or she was not at fault for causing the marriage to terminate and was the party initiating the divorce proceeding. Some of the harshest aspects of IMFA were tempered by amendments passed in 1990. Ironically, the government survey that elevated marriage fraud as a serious concern, and which spurred Congress to enact the law, was later held to be invalid and unreliable.[68]

6. The Immigration Act of 1990

The *Immigration Act of 1990* (IMMACT 90) brought both sweeping changes and technical revisions to many of the immigration laws at that time.[69] The ameliorative changes included relief for the family members—spouses and unmarried children—of those who legalized under the 1986 general amnesty or SAW programs. Titled "Family Unity," this program allowed those family

---

63 See, e.g., Donald Kerwin, "Lessons from IRCA for the House Judiciary Committee," *Huffington Post*, May 20, 2013, available at http://www.huffingtonpost.com/donald-kerwin/immigration-reform-and-control-act_b_3300045.html.

64 Immigration Marriage Fraud Amendments Act of 1986, 100 Stat. 3537, 3543.

65 INA §216.

66 INA §204(c).

67 *Bark v. INS*, 522 F.2d 1200 (9th Cir. 1975).

68 *Manwani v. INS*, 736 F. Supp. 1367 (W.D.N.C. 1990)

69 Immigration Act of 1990, 104 Stat. 4978.

members who were residing in the United States on the last day of registration for either of those programs to remain in the country and work legally in two-year increments until an immigrant visa was available for them.

Another benefit was the creation of Temporary Protected Status (TPS), which allowed the Justice Department to designate nationals from certain countries to be eligible for work authorization and protection from deportation. Designation for TPS was to be based on ongoing armed conflict, earthquake, flood, hurricane, or some other environmental disaster. Although the protections are temporary in nature, and do not lead to a permanent legal status, the program has allowed hundreds of thousands of nationals from Central America, Africa, and the Middle East to remain in the United States for long periods of time.

IMMACT 90 added more immigrant visas in both the employment- and family-based categories. It removed sexual preference as a ground of inadmissibility. In addition, it softened the harshest elements of IMFA by adding a waiver for those who were battered or subjected to mental cruelty by the U.S. citizen spouse. This form of relief would prove to be a prelude to much broader relief afforded to victims of domestic violence four years later. That legislation would grant victims the right to self-petition for permanent residence or use the abuse as relief to deportation.[70]

The more punitive aspects of IMMACT 90 included reduction in the forms of relief for those convicted of certain crimes, elimination of eligibility for asylum to those convicted of "aggravated felonies," and a five-year ban on various immigration benefits for those who failed to appear at their immigration hearing. The ban was later increased to ten years in the 1996 legislation.[71]

7. Illegal Immigration Reform and Immigrant Responsibility Act of 1996

By the mid-1990s, anti-immigrant sentiment had gained considerable momentum and support due to the failure of IRCA to control unauthorized immigration, the sense that the border was too porous, and an almost universal conclusion that the federal government needed to take corrective action. The 1993 bombing of the New York City World Trade Center by a group of (mostly) non-citizens intensified public opinion. Another important element

70 Violence Against Women Act, Pub. L. No. 103-322, tit. IV, 108 Stat. 1796, 1902–55.
71 INA § 240(b) (7).

was the growing influence of right-wing talk shows, restrictionist lobbying groups, and opportunistic politicians who portrayed unauthorized immigrants as a growing threat and used immigration as a wedge issue.

In California, the governor was reelected in 1994 due largely to the public outcry against images of Mexicans running through border checkpoints and across freeways to evade arrest, and to reports of what unauthorized immigrants cost the state in education and health care services. A state ballot measure which called for the expulsion of unauthorized children from elementary school and a prohibition on unauthorized immigrants' eligibility for state benefits and services won by a comfortable margin,[72] though it was unconstitutional and quickly enjoined by the federal courts.

By 1996, due in part to the popularity of the California ballot measure and political advocacy on the national level, the question was not whether Congress was going to pass punitive immigration legislation but how far it was going to go. Proposals included scaling back family-based immigration, eliminating any relief from removal, reducing eligibility for temporary benefits, and substantially beefing up border and interior enforcement. The result, the *Illegal Immigration Reform and Immigrant Responsibility Act* (IIRAIRA),[73] represented the harshest roll-back in rights and benefits in seventy years. Congress imposed strict income requirements on those petitioning for other family members, a one-year filing period for those seeking asylum, expedited removal of those who attempted to enter the United States with false documents or no documents, mandatory detention of those convicted of certain crimes or found to be inadmissible at the border, reduction in possible relief for those in removal proceedings, expansion of the crime-based grounds of inadmissibility and deportability, and limitations on judicial review.

One of the changes was the imposition of a three- or ten-year bar on admissibility for those who had acquired "unlawful presence" in the United States, which would be triggered by departing the country.[74] A waiver was available, but only if the applicant demonstrated extreme hardship to the U.S. citizen or LPR spouse or parent. Those who were required to leave the United States for consular processing were forced to wait abroad for up to a year while their waiver application was being adjudicated, with no guarantee it would ultimately be granted. Persons without immigration status who had

---

72 California Proposition 187, "Save Our State" (1994).
73 Illegal Immigration Reform and Immigrant Responsibility Act of 1996, 110 Stat. 3009.
74 INA § 212(a) (9) (B).

reentered or even attempted to reenter the United States after accruing one year of unlawful presence were required to remain outside the country for ten years before being eligible for a waiver.[75]

The result of these bars, in addition to heightened border enforcement, was to discourage or prevent the lawful reunification of close family members. Instead of leaving the country to attend an immigrant visa interview—and thus risking a potentially long absence—the family members of U.S. citizens and LPRs simply remained "caged" in the United States without immigration status. Unauthorized Mexican and Central Americans, who had been accustomed to traveling back and forth to their home countries, elected instead to remain in the United States without status. Many of them arranged to have their family members smuggled into the United States so they could all live together rather than returning to their home countries for periodic visits (Rosenblum 2012; Cornelius 2008).

It is ironic that one of the direct consequences of IIRAIRA, which was intended to discourage and punish unauthorized crossings, was to drive up the number of unauthorized persons permanently residing here. By 2005, the unauthorized population in the United States was estimated to be more than eleven million persons, and peaked at twelve million in 2007, almost 80 percent of whom came from Mexico or other Latin American countries (Passel and Cohn 2010, 1). Recent estimates of the unauthorized put the number at above eleven million.

8. Current U.S. Immigration Law and Policy

U.S. immigration policy represents the accumulation of Congressional action over the years. However, it is also manifested through trends and principles that infuse these laws since the federal government began asserting control in this area. Some of these principles date back more than two centuries: the establishment of grounds of exclusion and deportation, the enforcement of our borders, the assessment of fees from those seeking admission, and the assignment of financial responsibility on the person or company transporting the migrant to the United States. For example, most persons seeking admission are now "pre-screened" through the issuance of visas by consular officers abroad before they present themselves for admission; should the person be excluded, it is the airline company that is responsible for bearing the costs of

---

75 INA § 212(a) (9) (C) (i) (I).

his or her return. The "head taxes" of the early 1800s have ballooned into steep immigrant and non-immigrant visa fees that are intended to cover most of the costs of processing these applications. Border enforcement and the detention of those determined to be deportable is now a multibillion-dollar industry, involving thousands of border patrol agents, the construction of fortified fences, the use of sophisticated surveillance equipment, and, on any given day, the detention of approximately 34,000 aliens, translating to over 400,000 annually.

What emerges from the accretion of all these laws are certain principles or pillars on which the U.S. immigration system is built. These can be divided and classified in a number of ways, but four themes dominate: (1) restrictions on who can immigrate; (2) support for family unification; (3) encouragement of skilled laborers in need in the U.S. economy; and (4) protection for those fleeing persecution or domestic violence. The following is a brief analysis of each of these themes.

8.1 Immigration Restrictions

Most "immigration-related" funding goes to enforcing the law and restricting those who can immigrate to the United States. On March 1, 2003, the INS ceased to exist.[76] Its responsibilities were divided up and given to three new agencies within the Department of Homeland Security (DHS): U.S. Customs and Border Protection (CBP), which performs border enforcement and inspection functions, including determining the eligibility for admission of all noncitizens; U.S. Immigration and Customs Enforcement (ICE), which carries out interior enforcement, including the arrest, detention, and removal of those determined to be in the United States unlawfully; and U.S. Citizenship and Immigration Services (USCIS), which processes various immigration benefits.

Current funding levels of the CBP and the ICE total almost $18 billion. Their work is overwhelmingly devoted to protecting U.S. land and sea borders, inspecting non-citizens for their eligibility to enter the country, or internal enforcement and the removal of non-citizens. Congressional appropriations for the U.S. Border Patrol have risen from $232 million in 1989 to $3.8 billion in 2010. And the number of agents patrolling the border went up tenfold over the same period.

76 The Homeland Security Act of 2002, 116 Stat. 2135.

The United States has been steadily prioritizing border enforcement and the removal of unauthorized non-citizens for the past twenty-five years. Between 1988 and 1996, for example, the number of removals increased by 250 percent. In 1996, Congress passed the Antiterrorism and Effective Death Penalty Act[77] and the IIRAIRA,[78] both of which expanded the grounds of deportability and restricted eligibility for relief, causing the rate of removals to expand even further. This focus on exclusion and removal further accelerated after the September 11, 2001 terrorist attacks. During fiscal year (FY) 2013, ICE reported removing 368,644 aliens from the United States (U.S. Immigration and Customs Enforcement 2013). During the first five years of the Obama Administration, the United States deported nearly two million non-citizens, a staggering number when compared to the 2.3 million deported during the previous twenty years of Republican administrations.

In 2006, unable to reach consensus on broader immigration reform, Congress instead authorized construction of an 850-mile, double-layered fence along five important segments of the U.S.-Mexican border.[79] The following year it authorized reinforced fencing along 700 miles of border: approximately 650 miles have been constructed.

Programs such as Secure Communities, the Criminal Alien Program, and Section 287(g) coordinate the efforts of state and local criminal justice systems to identify and detain possible deportable immigrants. Increased prosecution of common immigration-related violations, such as reentry after deportation, has served to discourage repeat offenders. Moreover, smarter workplace enforcement, which has focused on auditing employers and levying fines rather than on conducting large-scale raids, has resulted in greater participation in the voluntary electronic employment verification system, E-Verify.

For the last twenty years, the enforcement approach has been termed "prevention through deterrence," which involves concentrating agents and surveillance mechanisms at heavily trafficked parts of the border. Unmanned aerial vehicle systems, remote video surveillance, ground sensors, and increased agents have lowered the success rate of unauthorized border crossers, pushed them into more remote areas of the desert, and forced them to rely on smugglers. But the border is still not "sealed," and may never be, for practical and economic reasons. Today it is estimated that approximately 300,000

---

77 Pub. L. No. 104-132, 110 Stat. 1214.
78 Pub. L. No. 104-208, div. C, 110 Stat. 3009, 3009-546 to 3009-724.
79 Secure Fence Act of 2006, Pub. Law 109-367, 120 Stat. 2638.

persons still find a way to cross without authorization each year, which is about equal to the number of unauthorized persons who return home (Passel and Cohn 2010).

The budget for the "benefits" side of the equation, the USCIS, is only $2.8 billion, or about five percent of the DHS budget. Most of the work of the USCIS is the adjudication of petitions and applications, such as for adjustment of status, asylum, or a family-based immigration status. However, a large part of the USCIS effort also goes to restricting immigration. The consular section of the Department of State (DOS) has jurisdiction over the adjudication of immigrant and non-immigrant visa applications from those filing abroad. In 2012, the DOS processed approximately 600,000 applications for an immigrant visa, and approved 482,000, or eighty percent. It also processed over eleven million applications for non-immigrant visas, and approved about nine million (DOS 2012).

The most common grounds of inadmissibility include the following categories: health-related; criminal-related; national security; public charge; fraud or false claims of citizenship; smuggling; unlawful presence, prior deportation, and other immigration violations; and various miscellaneous grounds.[80] In addition, each inadmissibility category is comprised of several subsections, so that the ten separate categories of inadmissibility actually include fifty-four different ways that an alien may be found inadmissible. These grounds overlap to some extent with the grounds of deportability, but there are separate ways—such as firearms violations and aggravated felonies—that an alien may be found deportable.[81]

As indicated previously, all of these grounds of inadmissibility and deportability have evolved over the years to where they now comprise a lengthy and complex set of restrictions. Beginning with Congressional authorization in 1989, detailed background checks are now performed on every adjustment of status or immigrant visa applicant, which involves the taking of biometrics, accessing FBI and other government records, and cross-checking against an Automated Biometric Identification System (IDENT) database containing almost 150 million fingerprints. Non-immigrant applicants are also subject to similar background checks and the storing of biographical information in an electronic U.S. Visitor and Immigrant Status Indicator Technology (US-VISIT) system, which tracks their entry and stay in the United States. Estimates are that

80 INA § 212(a).
81 INA § 237(a).

between one third and one half of the unauthorized persons residing in the United States entered legally and simply overstayed, hence the need for more accurate tracking. The collection of passengers' names on ship manifests 300 years ago has grown into a sophisticated business using the latest technology.

8.2 Family Reunification

Family unification has been a cornerstone of U.S. immigration law and policy since at least 1921, but it became the dominant purpose with the 1965 Immigration Act. In addition to scrapping the discriminatory national origin quotas and replacing them with one quota for Western Hemisphere and one for Eastern Hemisphere countries, the law expanded the number of visas available based on relationship to a U.S. citizen or LPR. The annual worldwide quota was raised to 290,000 visas, with the parents of U.S. citizens no longer subject to the quota. In addition, while half of the preference category visas were reserved for highly skilled immigrants under the prior law, the 1965 Act reduced that figure to twenty percent. In their place, family- based preference categories grew from representing half of the visas issued to almost seventy-five percent.

This change and prioritization has remained in place for the past forty-eight years. U.S. citizens have been able to petition for the following "immediate relatives," who enter or adjust status outside of the annual quota: spouses, unmarried children under twenty-one years of age, and parents (assuming the U.S. citizen petitioner is at least twenty-one years old). In FY 2012, approximately 480,000 visas were issued to immediate relatives and another 200,000 in the family-based preference categories. The following are the preference categories, the percent of visas allocated to each, and the number of visas issued during the last fiscal year: adult unmarried children of U.S. citizens (ten percent, 20,660 visas); spouses and unmarried children of LPRs (forty-nine percent, 99,709 visas); married children of U.S. citizens (eleven percent, 21,752 visas); and siblings of U.S. citizens (thirty percent, 202,019 visas). In 2012, a total of 680,000 visas were issued to applicants in the family-based categories, which represented two-thirds of all visas issued. Almost half of the total number of visas issued went to those who were not subject to the annual quota (DHS 2013, Table 6).

Legal immigration expanded after the 1965 Act from a quarter million immigrants annually in the 1950s to approximately one million by the late 1990s, where it has remained to the present time. Nevertheless, the countries of origin have also changed dramatically. During the 1950s, more than one-half of all legal immigration came from Europe, and one-half of those immigrants came from two countries: Germany and the United Kingdom. But while Europeans accounted for the bulk of the new immigrants fifty years ago, they now represent less than eight percent; more than eighty percent come from Mexico, other Latin American countries, and Asia (ibid., Table 2).

To demonstrate just how much change has occurred in the national origin make-up of current immigrants, one can look at the annual diversity visa lottery program, which was implemented in 1986 to reinvigorate immigration from Europe by increasing the admission of aliens from undersubscribed countries. Citizens from countries that used fewer than 50,000 immigrant visas during the prior five years qualify to apply. When the program was first implemented, 16,000 visas were set aside for applicants from Ireland. In 2012, almost all of the countries classified as European qualified to participate, representing twenty percent of those applicants who ultimately received diversity visas (ibid., Table 11). Thus, the region of the world that used to comprise almost all of the foreign born in the United States is now being encouraged to immigrate in order to "diversify" the U.S. population. The lifting of the national origin quotas in 1965, expansion of the total number of visas, and allowing more categories to enter outside the annual quota literally changed the face of the United States.

8.3 Immigration of Skilled Laborers

The 1990 Act did for employment-based immigration what the 1965 Act did for family unification. It increased the number of immigrant visas that could be issued every year based on employment skills to 140,000, which is approximately twenty percent of the current 675,000 annual quota. These fall into such categories as priority workers, professionals with advanced degrees, aliens with extraordinary ability, outstanding professors and researchers, multinational executives and managers, other skilled workers, and investors.

However, the more substantial change was in the increase in number and type of non-immigrant visas that could be issued. The 1990 Act authorized the admission of 131,000 "H" category non-immigrants, who qualify based on their having at least a bachelor's degree and an employer willing to sponsor them. The employer must offer them a job at a prevailing wage rate, but the employer does not need to recruit American workers or obtain a labor certificate. These workers may enter the United States for a three-year period, which can be extended for a total of six years; many H-1B workers go on to apply for permanent residence.

That year Congress also created four new non-immigrant classifications: "O" visas for those with extraordinary ability; "P" visas for internationally recognized athletes and entertainers, and artists in culturally unique programs; "Q" visas for workers in cultural exchange programs; and "R" visas for workers in religious occupations.

In FY 2011, the USCIS recorded about fifty-three million admissions to persons entering on non-immigrant visas and who were issued a formal arrival/departure document (Form I-94). Of that figure, the overwhelming majority (more than forty million) were admitted as "visitors for pleasure" ("B-2" visas). Most of the rest were admitted as temporary visitors for business (5.5 million), diplomats (378,000), exchange visitors (527,000), and temporary workers and their families (3.3 million). Thus, the number entering for business purposes was approximately ten million, or twenty percent of the total non-immigrants admitted with I-94s.

However, the current law does not allow for a sufficient number of low-skilled immigrant workers. Currently, only 10,000 visas are set aside for this category, a third of which typically go to Mexicans. The H-2A program, which allows for the admission of agricultural and other low-skilled non-immigrant workers, is bureaucratically unwieldy, demanding, and not responsive to employers' needs for seasonal workers.

Along with providing a variety of ways to immigrate or enter the United States on a temporary visa, current law also includes labor protections for U.S. workers. As indicated earlier, most employment-based immigrant visa applications are conditioned upon the Department of Labor (DOL) certifying that U.S. workers are not able or available to perform the specified job duties. The DOL's Employment and Training Administration uses a Program Electronic Review Management (PERM), computerized system to scan attestation forms filed by employers regarding their compliance with all regulatory requirements. Even H-1B applicants must attest that the employer is paying the prevailing wage; that he or she will not adversely affect the working conditions of similarly employed workers; that there is no strike, lockout, or work stoppage going on; and that the employer has posted a notice of the hiring of the H-1B worker.

8.4 Humanitarian Relief

Modern U.S. refugee policy began in the aftermath of World War II, with the adoption of formal definitions of "refugee" and "displaced person," the funding of voluntary agencies (VOLAGS) to process and resettle persons who were determined unable to return to their homeland, and the passage of legislation allowing for the admission of designated war victims.[82]   The admission of displaced persons occurred outside the annual quota system and during the four-year period from 1948-1952, more than 400,000 were resettled in the United States from parts of Europe and the Soviet bloc. A subsequent law in 1953 authorized the admission of another 200,000 "refugees," "escapees," or "German expellees."[83]

Despite its restrictionist tone and purpose, the *McCarran-Walter Act of 1952* contained a provision allowing the Attorney General to parole an unlimited number of persons "for emergency reasons deemed strictly in the public interest."[84] This broad parole authority allowed for the entry of over a million immigrants prior to the establishment of the U.S. refugee program in 1980.

As explained earlier, the 1965 Act ended the system of national origin quotas and replaced it with two hemispheric caps. It also specifically authorized the admission of refugees from communist or communist-dominated countries or from the Middle East, albeit as part of the world-wide quota.

One of the longest and most generous "refugee" programs has been directed towards Cubans fleeing that country since the late-1950s. Up until 1965 they were allowed to enter without any numerical restriction. Beginning in 1966, if they were able to make it to U.S. shores they were formally paroled into the country and allowed to adjust status after one year. In 1980, during a 162-day period, approximately 125,000 Cubans (called *Marielitos* due to the Cuban port from which most of them left) were paroled into the United States. Since the Cuban exodus began in 1958, an estimated one million Cubans have been allowed to immigrate to the United States.

The other major country benefiting from the U.S. refugee admission policy has been Vietnam. From the mid-1970s through the late 1990s, more than

---

82 See Displaced Persons Act of 1948, 62 Stat. 1009; Displaced Persons Act of 1950, 64 Stat. 219.

83 Refugee Relief Act of 1953, 67 Stat. 400.

84 INA § 212(d)(5) (1952).

1.1 million Southeast Asian refugees were admitted. The vast majority were from Vietnam, with a much smaller number from Cambodia and Laos. When one factors in the derivative family members and the children fathered by U.S. servicemen, the number is closer to 1.6 million entering as a result of the war in Vietnam.

The *Refugee Act of 1980* attempted to regularize refugee admission by setting an annual limit of 50,000 and establishing formal procedures and funding for their resettlement.[85] It brought the United States into compliance with the 1951 Convention and the 1957 Protocol. It established the definition of "refugee" based on the Convention definition that is applied today, namely those residing in a third country that are unwilling to return based on "persecution, or a well-founded fear of persecution, on account of race, religion, nationality, membership in a particular social group, or political opinion."[86] However, even more significant was the application of this definition to those persons already in the United States, who could apply for "asylum." Such applicants could be residing in the United States with or without status, or could have been paroled in to apply for this benefit. One year after being admitted as a refugee or granted asylum, the refugee or asylee may apply for permanent residency. In 2012, over 150,000 refugees and asylees were granted LPR status, a number that operates outside the strict annual quota system.

One of the goals of the Refugee Act was to apply uniform standards to those who qualified for refugee or asylum status, and to decouple that determination from U.S. foreign policy. The Act prohibited discrimination based on the applicant's race or country of origin. Implementation of the Act during the first few years, however, continued to reflect an ideological bias. Most applicants for asylum during the 1980s came from Haiti or Central American countries with which the United States maintained close political ties. U.S. officials resisted the formal findings that citizens of allied countries were suffering political persecution. Reform came in the 1990s due to litigation and other political pressures, and resulted in the creation of a separate division of trained asylum adjudicators who apply neutral standards.

Another group that has received special humanitarian treatment is victims of domestic violence. Over the past two decades, Congress has become increasingly aware of the special vulnerability of these persons and has implemented a number of special forms of immigration relief for them.

85 94 Stat. 102.
86 INA § 101(a)(42).

Beginning in 1994, with passage of the Violence Against Women Act (VAWA), persons who are married to a U.S. citizen or an LPR have been able to "self-petition" for permanent resident status if their spouse physically or mentally abused them.[87] The same relief is available to the children of abusive parents. Aliens in removal proceedings can apply for a separate form of relief, VAWA cancellation of removal, if they have been physically present in the United States for three continuous years, demonstrate good moral character, and show proof of abuse by the citizen or LPR spouse. In 2012, over 4,500 victims of abuse were granted LPR status based on VAWA protections.

In addition, Congress has also added three other forms of relief for victims of abuse and crime, even though they are not related to U.S. citizens or LPRs. These include T non-immigrant status for victims of severe forms of human trafficking; U non-immigrant status for persons who have suffered substantial harm as a result of being the victim of certain listed crimes; and Special Immigrant Juvenile Status for children found dependent on a juvenile court. Almost 5,000 persons were granted permanent residency in 2012 under these provisions, while thousands more were granted temporary status.

9. Proposed Changes to Immigration Law

Starting shortly after passage of the 1996 law, immigrant rights advocates began looking for ways to soften the legislation's harshest effects, as did growers and other employers who were feeling the sting of workplace enforcement and a shortage of skilled U.S. workers. They began in earnest in 2006 and again the following year to marry the opposing interests of increased border protection with an earned pathway to legalization for the estimated eleven million unauthorized workers. Those efforts failed, but they led to a blueprint for legislation that was offered by a bipartisan group of Senators in April 2013.[88]

While not likely to become law in its current form, the Senate bill (S. 744) demonstrates the delicate and complex balance of competing interests and provisions involved in a "comprehensive" approach to reform. The bill provides for stepped-up border enforcement; mandatory electronic employment verification; increased visas for those with degrees in science, math, technology and engineering (STEM) fields; streamlined procedures for agricultural employers seeking a reliable supply of low-skilled workers; labor protections for domestic workers; and a pathway to citizenship for the

87 108 Stat. 1796.

88 Border Security, Economic Opportunity, and Immigration Modernization Act, S.744.

unauthorized. Passage of such legislation depends on the support of a diverse group of members and special interest groups, any of whom might withdraw their support if the bill is substantially amended.

The enforcement elements of those bills would expand fencing and surveillance, as well as increase the number of border agents. The 2013 bill would also establish "triggers" that would have to be met before the immigration benefits would be implemented. The bill calls for the submission to Congress of border security and fencing strategies that would be funded with an additional $4.5 billion. As currently drafted, the bill would require DHS to stop nine in ten unauthorized border crossers—achieve a "ninety percent effectiveness rate"—across the U.S.-Mexico border. If this rate is not achieved, then an advisory commission would be created and $2 billion in additional funding would be authorized for more border officers, infrastructure, and technology. The bill also calls for phased-in implementation of a mandatory electronic employment verification system (E-Verify) to be used by all U.S. employers, and another electronic system to identify those entering the country by air or sea. All non-citizens allowed to work would be issued a biometric work authorization card that bears the person's photograph. Prospective employers would be required to verify that the person's photo matches the photograph stored in the national computerized system.

Once the border strategy has begun, DHS would implement a multi-year registration program to legalize the millions of unauthorized workers who are not eligible for any other benefits under the proposed law. They would first register for provisional immigrant (RPI) status, which would entitle them to employment authorization and protection from deportation. After six years in RPI status, they would need to renew it; after ten years they would be eligible to apply for permanent resident status, assuming the border protection effectiveness rate has been achieved and triggers have been pulled. Finally, after three years in LPR status, they could apply for citizenship. Eligibility for RPI status would be dependent on proving physical presence in the United States on a fixed date, continuous residence since that date, and not having been convicted of certain criminal offenses.

Those granted RPI status would be able to apply for their spouses and children if they were also present in the United States on a fixed date. Eligibility for renewed RPI and the later LPR status would require payment of steep fees and penalties, payment of back taxes, proof of having been steadily employed, proof of income at 125 percent of the poverty line, and proof of pursuing a course of study in English and U.S. history and civics.

Agricultural workers would be eligible to apply for legal status under a separate program. Those who can demonstrate having worked a certain number of hours in agricultural labor during a prior two-year period would be entitled to a "blue card" that would authorize them to work. If they continued to work in farm labor a certain number of hours over the next five years, they would qualify to apply for LPR status.

The 2013 bill would also represent an important shift from prioritizing family-based immigration, which now represents seventy-five percent of lawful immigration, toward one that favors skills, advanced degrees, and work experience, which over time would represent about half of all immigrant visas. It would create a new "merit-based" system allowing for the granting of 120,000 immigrant visas—increasing annually to a cap of 250,000—contingent on the unemployment rate remaining under 8.5 percent. These visas would be given out on a point-based system similar to one used in Canada that considers the applicant's education, employment skills, and the needs of employers. More visas would be available to those with degrees in STEM fields, as well as for foreign doctors and other professionals. Almost twice as many non-immigrant visas would be available for those in the H-1B category, and entrepreneurs would be provided with "start-up" visas if they plan to form their own companies.

A second merit-based system would favor length of time residing in the United States and time waiting in backlogged visa categories, rather than employment skills. A new "W" non-immigrant visa category would be created for low-skilled, low-wage workers who would be employed by registered employers in occupations that have experienced labor shortages. These workers would first be admitted or granted temporary status in three-year increments with the possibility of it leading to LPR status. This reflects the need for a more flexible legal immigration system where low-skilled workers can enter legally to fill temporary jobs, and in turn should reduce the flow of unauthorized entries.

In contrast, the bill would phase out the fourth preference, family-based visa category—siblings of U.S. citizens—and those married children over age thirty-one of U.S. citizens in the third preference category. The fourth preference accounts for about 60,000 visas, or almost thirty percent of those issued every year in the family-based preference categories. But this reduction in visas would be offset by the elimination after ten years of all family-based backlogs. Certain preference categories for applicants from Mexico and the Philippines have become so backlogged that if they applied for a visa today in the third or fourth preference they would die long before the visa became available. There are now approximately 4.4 million persons waiting in line for a family- or employment-based visa to become current, so the elimination of the backlog in 2023 would signify a tremendous benefit to a large portion of that applicant pool. Another significant change would be the re-classification of the second preference F-2A category—spouses and children under age twenty-one of LPRs—to immediate relatives, thus making them eligible for a visa outside the annual worldwide quota system.

Conclusion

A variety of factors—unemployment rates, racial biases, religious intolerance, political ideologies, nativist sentiments, foreign threats, labor needs, and the demands of the global marketplace—have all played a role in shaping U.S. immigration laws and policies. So has the nation's underlying commitment to supporting freedom, human rights, family reunification, and the protection of laborers. It is within this clash of often conflicting priorities that immigration proposals are debated, modified, defeated or enacted, and implemented.

If immigration has served a vital role in shaping the United States as a nation, it is also a hotly-contested and divisive issue. Forty-three million foreign-born persons—and perhaps nearly an equal number of their children—reside in the United States. The foreign-born comprise fifteen percent of its workforce. Throughout U.S. history, politicians have repeatedly used the issue of immigration to either stir up anti-immigrant sentiments or appeal to an important part of the electorate. The debate over the pros and cons of U.S. immigration policies is as old, if not older, than the founding of the country. Today we are witnessing simply another chapter in this long narrative. The unusual alignment of business, labor, religious groups, and pro-immigrant forces are pitted against "enforcement-first" supporters, nativists, and skeptics who see no advantage in rewarding anyone who is here unlawfully. Public sentiment, as well as the rising political influence of the foreign-born, seems to favor passage of a comprehensive bill that would address all of these concerns. However, history has also shown us how difficult it is to reach a consensus and to predict the outcome of a debate infused with deep-seated emotions.

References

Cornelius, Wayne. 2008. "Reforming the Management of Migration Flows from Latin America to the United States." San Diego, CA: Center for Comparative Immigration Studies. http://ccis.ucsd.edu/wp-content/uploads/2009/07/WP-170.pdf.

Hutchinson, Edward Prince. 1981. *Legislative History of American Immigration Policy 1798-1965*. Philadelphia, PA: University of Pennsylvania Press.

Kerwin, Donald. 2010. "More than IRCA: US Legalization Programs and the Current Policy Debate." Washington, D.C.: Migration Policy Institute.

Motomura, Hiroshi. 1996. *Americans in Waiting: The Lost Story of Immigration and Citizenship in the United States*. Oxford: Oxford University Press.

Passel, Jeffrey, and D'Vera Cohn. 2010. *U.S Unauthorized Immigration Flows Are Down Sharply Since Mid-Decade*. Washington, DC: Pew Hispanic Center.

Robertson, Craig. 2010. *The Passport in America*. Oxford: Oxford University Press.

Rosenblum, Marc. 2012. "Border Security: Immigration Enforcement between Ports of Entry." Washington, D.C.: Congressional Research Service. http://fpc.state.gov/documents/organization/180681.pdf.

Rosenfeld, Richard N. 1996. *American Aurora: A Democratic-Republican Returns; The Sup pressed History of Our Nation's Beginnings and the Heroic Newspaper That Tried to Report It*. New York, NY: St. Martin's Griffin.

DHS (U.S. Department of Homeland Security). 2013. *Yearbook of Immigration Statistics: 2012*. http://www.dhs.gov/yearbook-immigration-statistics-2012-legal-permanent-residents.

DOS (U.S. Department of State). 2012. "Immigrant and Nonimmigrant Visa Ineligibilities for FY 2012." Washington, D.C: DOS.

ICE (U.S. Immigration and Customs Enforcement). 2013. "FY 2013 ICE Immigration Removals." Washington, D.C.: ICE. http://www.ice.gov/doclib/about/offices/ero/pdf/2013-ice-immigration-removals.pdf.

CHAPTER III

The Influence of Civil Society in U.S. Immigrant Communities and the U.S. Immigration Debate

Sara Campos

Introduction

In his November 2012 acceptance speech after being elected to a second term in office, President Barack Obama promised to press for comprehensive immigration reform (CIR) (Bennett, Becerra and Lauter 2012). It was a commitment he had made prior to his first election and one that remained unfulfilled. The audience nevertheless cheered and shortly after the election, CIR returned to the forefront of the political agenda. An elusive goal for over a decade, CIR was suddenly on the table. Immigration advocates in Washington, D.C. likened the palpable, almost overnight shift to the change from black and white to color in the movie the Wizard of Oz.

For at least the last decade, Americans have been faced with an increasingly intractable problem—what to do with the estimated eleven to twelve million people who live in an unauthorized status in the United States. These immigrants contribute their labor and help businesses thrive, but reap few gains.[1] Many work in an underground economy and live in fear that, at any moment, federal agents might whisk them away from the United States and separate them from their families.

How has civil society handled this issue and can it supply any solutions? This chapter discusses civil society in the context of immigration policy, reviews the history of civil society's growth and trajectory in this area, and discusses the sectors most involved in serving immigrants and shaping immigration policy.

1. How is Civil Society Defined and Who Are the Actors in the Immigration Field?

No universally accepted definition of "civil society" exists (Banulescu-Bogdan 2011, 2). In fact, the term is often defined by what it is not rather than what it is. It has been described as "an area of association and action independent of the state and the market in which citizens can organize and pursue purposes that are important to them, individually and collectively (Teegen, Doh and Vachani 2004).

Most working definitions build on the premise that civil society consists of social groups and relationships outside of government or public

---

1 Unauthorized immigrants are eligible for emergency health care and can attend public elementary and high school, but receive few additional benefits.

administration" (Persell 1997). These groups include families, communities, religious organizations, ethnic groups, schools, neighborhoods, sports leagues, labor unions, parent-teacher associations and a myriad of other voluntary associations in which people formally and informally engage. A signature quality of U.S. civil society is its independence from the government.

Political theorists see civil society as a pivotal arena for the construction and articulation of ideas, projects, and social movements (Cohen and Arato 1992). Civil society encompasses the myriad non-state actors that formally and informally influence immigration-related rules, practices, and processes, and that deliver services to and advocate for immigrants. These include non-governmental organizations (NGOs), professional associations, religious and faith-based institutions, trade unions, charities, women's networks, advocacy groups, philanthropies, civic engagement fora, chambers of commerce, and other stakeholders.

Some of these organizations, like the American Friends Service Center (AFSC), were founded almost a century ago. Others, like the New Orleans Worker Center for Racial Justice and the Alabama Coalition for Immigrant Justice, are relative newcomers. Civil society groups differ considerably, both in membership and ideology. They include grassroots entities such as the National Day Laborer Organizing Network (NDLON), a coalition that links over 40 casual and day laborer and worker centers; the American Immigration Lawyers Association (AILA), a professional group that counts among its clients and constituents firms that handle high-tech visas for the California Silicon Valley; and the varied non-profits and ministries that serve immigrants and pursue policy reform under the auspices of the Catholic Church. Although these groups hold diverse interests, they generally favor increased protections for immigrants and legalization for the unauthorized.

Civil society also includes groups that seek to limit immigration and immigration levels and seek expansion and vigorous enforcement of law.[2] These actors and organizations include scholars concerned with a perceived lack of assimilation, like Samuel Huntington, think tanks such as the Center for Immigration Studies and the Heritage Foundation, and advocacy organizations

2 It is not obvious that restrictionist organizations should invariably be included in the definition of "civil society." Some scholars define civil society as agents that adhere to the protection of all members of society. To the extent a restrictionist organization seeks to curtail the rights of immigrants, particularly with illegal or violent means, it may exist on the borders of this definition.

such as the Federation for American Immigration Reform (FAIR).

Thus, immigration policy exists in a tensive dynamic of competing and multi-layered interests. The opposing camps have grown and shifted over time, arriving at a stalemate over CIR. However, there are signs that the terrain has shifted slightly. Demographic growth and voting patterns of Latinos and Asians have strengthened immigration advocates and weakened the restrictionist movement. In addition, select states and localities have promoted immigrant integration and a less public dialogue between immigrants and native born Americans has diffused tensions, potentially paving the way for more significant change.

2. How Civil Society Has Shaped Immigration Policy: Historical Touchstones

2.1 Immigration Prior to the Passage of the Immigration Reform and Control Act

Americans have long demonstrated ambivalence towards immigration, often vacillating between the humanitarian values emblazoned on the statue of liberty and anxieties over the impact of newcomers on employment and national security (Tichenor 1994). Immigration policy is also highly susceptible to foreign and economic concerns. In times of abundance, the country has welcomed or at least tolerated immigrants; in less prosperous times, policies have become more exclusionary.

Negative perceptions of immigrants have seeped into the body politic for more than a century. At least since the 1880s, the notion that immigrants steal jobs from native workers, depress wages, add to the ranks of the native poor, and compete for education, health, and other social services have been common themes (Espenshade 1992). Negative sentiments towards immigrants arose with each new wave of newcomers that arrived in the United States, including the Irish, Germans, and Italians. Latinos, Asians, Middle Easterners and South Asians have now taken their place (Scribner 2013).

For almost two centuries, pockets of civil society have voiced concerns over immigrants. This occurred in the mid-1800s as the "American" and "Know Nothing" parties rallied against Irish immigrants fleeing the potato famine, as well as against Germans, Poles and other groups. The Catholic Church, a recipient of such animus, was an early defender of immigrants. It ministered to them through its parishes, settlement houses, hospitals, grade schools, high schools and universities, and social service programs (ibid.). In 1921, the U.S. Catholic Bishops created a Bureau of Immigration to organize and unify its response to immigrant services and advocacy (ibid.).

Hostilities towards immigrants surged in the latter part of the nineteenth century as immigration from Europe doubled in size and changed in character from Western, to Eastern and Southern European immigrants. In response, Congress passed a series of measures aimed at controlling entry into the country (Tichenor 1994). These included the *Chinese Exclusion Act of 1882,* which prohibited Chinese immigration and banned the naturalization of Chinese nationals. By the turn of the century, Congress had also passed a bill imposing a literacy test that would have required immigrants to demonstrate the ability to read and write in English or some other language. Presidents Cleveland, Taft, and Wilson vetoed the law, but in 1917, Congress overrode the veto (Espenshade 1992).

Organized labor was deeply divided over the issue, but prominent labor leader Samuel Gompers ultimately embraced the tests (Burgoon et al. 2010). On the other hand, working through its war relief agency, the Catholic Church condemned the tests. This agency later became the National Catholic Welfare Conference (NCWC).

Anxieties over immigration continued into the new century and grew to such an extent that by the early 1920s, Congress enacted the first law that restricted immigration numerically (Tichenor 1994). The law limited the annual number of immigrants who could be admitted from any country to two percent of the number of people from that country who already resided in the United States as of 1890. The NCWC opposed the new quota law, while organized labor supported it.

The Great Depression and the quota law significantly reduced immigration into the United States (Espenshade 1992). By the 1940s, the United States had abolished the Chinese Exclusion Act and instituted the *Bracero* program, a system that brought Mexican and Caribbean workers to work on U.S. Western farms. The program did little to stem the flow of unauthorized immigration and may have even sparked more immigration: by the 1950s, unauthorized immigration was on the rise again (Tichenor 1994). By 1954, the problem was deemed so serious that the U.S. Border Patrol launched Operation Wetback, deporting more than one million unauthorized Mexican immigrants together with numerous U.S. citizens (ibid.). As a result, immigration lessened immediately, but because of continuing labor needs as well as loopholes in a 1952 Immigration Law that did not penalize employers who hired them, unauthorized immigrants continued to arrive.[3]

In 1964, with a magnified lens on civil rights, a coalition of leaders from labor, the Catholic Church, and civil rights and ethnic groups, protested the abuses of the *Bracero* program and successfully lobbied to abolish it. In 1965, the same coalition of faith, labor, and civil rights leaders advocated that Congress dismantle the quota system and establish new pathways for legal immigration. The family preference system that was enacted by the resulting law is still in place today (Bacon 2012). However, the 1965 Act did little to stem the flow of unauthorized immigrants: over the following decade, apprehensions of the unauthorized totaled 8.3 million (Tichenor 1994).

By the late 1970s, public disquiet over the increasing number of unauthorized immigrants had significantly increased and in 1977 Carter turned to Congress to pass legislation that would add 2,000 new border patrol agents to the U.S.-Mexico border, impose civil and criminal penalties on employers that hired unauthorized immigrants, and allow unauthorized immigrants to legalize their status (Chishti et al. 2011). Congress refused to take up the legislation, but the following year it established the Select Commission on Immigration and Refugee Policy (SCRIP), installing Reverend Theodore Hesburgh, the president of Notre Dame University, as its chairman. Among other ideas, the Commission recommended employer sanctions and a one-time amnesty program to legalize unauthorized immigrants. These recommendations were later incorporated in the *Immigration Reform and Control Act of 1986* (IRCA).

2.2 The Immigrant Reform and Control Act of 1986

Congress debated IRCA for several years before sending it to President Reagan for his signature. It consisted of four main provisions: employer sanctions that penalized employers who hired unauthorized workers; legalization for unauthorized immigrants who had either resided in the United States for a certain period or had performed farm labor; a guest worker program; and increased border enforcement.

---

3 The 1952 Immigration Law instituted penalties for harboring unauthorized workers, but carved out an exception to protect Texas agricultural interests. The measure exempting growers from these penalties came to be known as the Texas Proviso.

IRCA's provisions appear like a prism that changes depending on one's perspective. To restrictionists, the bill's legalization provisions appeared excessively generous and scornful of rule of law concerns. To some immigrant advocates, IRCA represented a watershed moment of a different kind, criminalizing work for the first time, creating another *Bracero* program, and militarizing the border. Like many hotly contested compromises, IRCA was opposed and supported by both liberals and conservatives.

The main trade union federation to which most U.S. unions belong, the American Federation of Labor-Congress of Industrial Organizations (AFL-CIO), supported employer sanctions based on the belief that they would stop unauthorized immigration and stem job competition from unauthorized immigrants (Bacon 2012). The U.S. Catholic Conference gave IRCA mixed support. It opposed sanctions, but supported a broad amnesty program (Espenshade 1992).

Groups like the National Council of La Raza (NCLR) and the Mexican American Legal Defense and Education Fund (MALDEF) opposed IRCA. They believed sanctions would result in discrimination against Latinos and others who looked and sounded foreign. Together with a coalition of civil rights organizations that included African American groups and the American Civil Liberties Union (ACLU), they mounted a vigorous campaign against employer sanctions (Fuchs 1993).

Surprisingly, unlike other periods of American history, very little xenophobic enmity reared its head during the IRCA debate. A few groups concerned with the environment such as Zero Population and a relatively new organization, the Federation for American Immigration Reform (FAIR) (later joined by the Center for Immigration Studies) opposed IRCA, but they did not carry the day. Neither did a few small organizations on the left. On November 6, 1986, with the support of free-market conservatives, IRCA passed the 99th Congress.[4]

Although a coalition of faith, civil rights and ethnic groups waged a powerful campaign against IRCA, their reach beyond Washington was fairly limited. This changed with the passage of the new legislation. New organizations sprouted to meet the needs of new applicants. Because the law's sponsors were concerned that potential beneficiaries would fear applying with the federal

---

4 Pub. L. 99–603, 100 Stat. 3359 (November 6, 1986).

government, it selected local groups around the country to act as "qualified designated entities" (QDEs). QDEs were charged with assisting legalization applicants in completing their applications and submitting them to the federal government. The US Catholic bishops mobilized the largest network of QDEs in the country. Many former QDEs continue to provide services today, albeit as tax-exempt charitable immigration programs (Kerwin 2006).

In addition to government-sponsored QDEs, private philanthropies began investing in the immigrant rights field. They believed that the government was not adequately prepared for the immense task of legalizing the eligible population (Freedberg and Wang 2008). In 1981, the Ford Foundation provided seed money to establish the National Immigration Forum. It also funded immigrant rights coalitions in New York, Boston, Chicago, Los Angeles, and San Francisco—cities in five states where immigrants were heavily concentrated. These coalitions drew from a wide array of grassroots, faith and ethnic-based organizations in their communities and also became members of the board of directors of the Forum. This newly formed infrastructure was centrally based in Washington, D.C., but also radiated out to local organizations. Additional coalitions were later established in San Diego, South Florida and elsewhere.

Nearly three million people obtained legal status under IRCA. The unauthorized population dropped following implementation of the law (Baker 1997). However, within a few years, the numbers of unauthorized migrants began to rise again. Scholars offer several reasons for this increase (Tichenor 1994). As immigrants became lawful permanent residents (LPRs), they sought to legalize their family members through the normal immigration process, but because of caps imposed by the quota system, some individuals had to wait years to legalize. As a result, many family members opted to enter without status.

The continued demand for low-skilled workers led to a surge in the unauthorized population in the 1990s (ibid.). IRCA supporters had argued that the law's employer sanctions provisions, combined with increased border enforcement, would stem illegal immigration. However, reports by the Rand Corporation and Urban Institute noted that the employer sanctions measures proved difficult to enforce (Fix 1991).

Adding to the growing number of economic migrants was an influx of refugees fleeing civil war and turmoil in Central America and the Caribbean. A vast number of them found it impossible to obtain legal visas and crossed the U.S. border surreptitiously.[5] Due to the prevailing politics of the Reagan and Bush years, the majority of Guatemalans, Salvadorans, and Haitians who applied for asylum received denials during this period.[6] These negative decisions spurred the rise of what was later called the "sanctuary movement." Moved by the testimonies of refugees, faith-based groups sought to protect them and zealously fought the government's blanket disapproval of their asylum claims (Gzesh 2006).

The movement included over 150 congregations that openly defied the government's policy by publicly sponsoring and supporting unauthorized Central American refugees (ibid.). About 1,000 Christian Churches and Jewish Synagogues endorsed the concept and practice of sanctuary. Members of the new immigrant coalitions founded after IRCA and an increasing number of activists who sought an end to military aid in El Salvador joined the sanctuary churches. Lawyers began forming *pro bono* panels to represent refugees in various cities around the country. Many of them established precedent setting cases based on the relatively new *Refugee Act of 1980* (ibid.). In addition, Central American refugees formed mutual assistance organizations that provided food, legal advice, health care and information about conditions in their home countries. Many of these programs survive today.

The U.S. government began charging people who had been protecting refugees with harboring unauthorized immigrants. The trials generated substantial publicity and resulted in split verdicts. Subsequently, the National Lawyers Guild, ACLU, and Center for Constitutional Rights filed a national class action lawsuit contending that the government's application of immigration laws violated the First Amendment, equal protection and due process clauses of the U.S. Constitution.[7] The plaintiff sanctuary churches argued that asylum determinations had to be made on a non-discriminatory basis without regard to ideology or foreign policy considerations. The court dismissed most of the plaintiffs' claims except the one concerning equal protection.

---

5 When Congress passed the Refugee Act in 1980, it brought U.S. law into compliance with international human rights standards, specifically the 1951 United Nations Convention and the 1967 Protocol Relating to the Status of Refugees. However, the Act did not provide a mechanism for individuals to apply for asylum within their countries or outside the United States.

6 In 1984, approval rates for Salvadoran and Guatemalan asylum cases were under three percent. That same year, the approval rate for Iranians was sixty percent, forty percent for Afghans fleeing the Soviet invasion, and thirty-two percent for Poles (Gzesh 2006).

7 *American Baptist Churches v. Thornburgh*, 666 F. Supp.1358 (N.D. Cal. 1987).

Immigrant rights advocacy involving faith-based groups, lawyers, and the refugees themselves, ultimately resulted in changing the government's stance on Central American refugees. After extensive discovery, the government settled the *American Baptist Churches v. Thornburgh* case (the *ABC* case) and permitted Salvadoran and Guatemalan asylum seekers to re-adjudicate their claims (Blum 1991). The settlement dovetailed with regulations establishing a new corps of specially trained asylum officers. Prior to the settlement, INS personnel were charged with deciding asylum cases. Because they also enforced immigration laws, they reviewed asylum claims through an enforcement lens.

At about the same time, Congress enacted the *Immigration Act of 1990* (IMMACT).[8] Among other provisions, IMMACT created a new program called Temporary Protected Status (TPS). TPS authorized the Attorney General to allow individuals to remain in the United States if their countries were engaged in armed conflict or experienced a natural disaster or another extraordinary situation that endangered their lives. The law mandated protection for Salvadorans. Due to the *ABC* case settlement and new regulations, Salvadoran asylum seekers finally obtained the refuge they had sought.

Yet as the sanctuary coalitions pursued and savored these gains, the unauthorized population surged again. By 1993, migrant apprehensions had risen to 1.3 million, a figure equal to that of 1985, the year preceding IRCA's passage (Tabirian 2013).

2.3 The 1990s Backlash

Early in President William Clinton's tenure as president, a confluence of events combined with the economic insecurities of a recession once again placed the immigration issue, and particularly asylum, in the headlines. Two of the president-elect's proposed attorney generals, both women, revealed they had employed unauthorized nannies and, as a result, had to withdraw from consideration (Gonzalez 1993). The issue reminded a wary electorate of the U.S. reliance on authorized immigrants.

In the meantime, new asylum procedures required by the *ABC* settlement were being administered. When the newly trained asylum officers arrived, they inherited a backlog of 114,000 asylum applications cases, and the number of applications continued to increase. From 1968 to 1975, the United States averaged only 200 applications per year. By 1993, the number of applications

8 Pub. L. 101-649, 104 Stat. 4978 (November. 29, 1990).

swelled to about 150,000 (Conover 1993). Those who applied under the new system and were not deportable were often given work authorization. Thus, according to critics, the backlog attracted spurious claims (ibid.). Moreover, the kinds of clear adjudications that had been decided during the Cold War years gave way to far more complex claims arising from troubled pockets throughout the globe.

In the fall of 1991, a military coup ousted Father Jean Bertrand Aristide, a Catholic priest who had won the support of sixty-seven percent of the electorate, most of whom came from impoverished neighborhoods of Port-au-Prince. After the coup, military leaders waged a reign of terror against Aristide supporters. In the brutal aftermath, thousands of Haitians took to the high seas in rickety boats to seek asylum in Miami and elsewhere. The new asylum officers adjudicated the claims of those who were found to have a credible fear of returning to Haiti and who were screened into the United States from Guantánamo Naval Base (Immigration and Refugee Board of Canada 1992).

In February 1993, a truck bomb detonated below the North Tower of the World Trade Center, killing six people and injuring hundreds. One of the co-conspirators in the bombing had applied for asylum and absconded. It was later learned that he and others had been followers of the radical cleric Sheik Omar Abdel-Rahman who had also sought asylum (Treaster 1993; Bernstein 1993).

Later that same year, a ship called the *Golden Venture* ran aground in New York Harbor with almost three hundred Chinese immigrants (Conover 1993). Most of them were natives of the Fujian Province of China fleeing the country's one-child population policy. Although some passengers had valid claims, many who arrived during the period admitted that they received coaching by their smugglers to claim they were fleeing China's one-child policy (Kung 2000).

Taken alone, these incidents would have attracted attention, but might not have led to negative public perceptions of the asylum system. But given the economic insecurities of the day, and spurred by the restrictionist lobby, the press devoted considerable coverage to the asylum issue and the notion that the United States had lost control of its borders (Weiner 1993). Books, articles and journals titled "Immigration: R.I.P" or worse became commonplace (Clad 1994; Curtis 1993).

Congress considered numerous reform bills during this period. Divisions within civil society had sharpened considerably. On one side were clusters of media and politically-savvy restrictionists riding a wave of discontent and urging Congress to tighten the asylum system, among other proposals. On the other side was a broad coalition of pro-immigrant advocates consisting of national organizations and ethnic and faith-based groups. Some of these groups had worked together prior to the passage of IRCA and during the struggles of Central American asylum-seekers in the United States. They attempted to respond to the media frenzy and presented former asylum clients who might have been sent to death squads if more restrictive congressional reforms had been instituted as proposed.

Throughout the period, Catholic bishops repeatedly criticized the increasingly restrictionist approach to immigration policy. In 1993, the U.S. Catholic Conference expressed concern over the animosity "toward immigrants evident now in some parts of society and even, sad to say, supported by public officials," and it rejected policies that (it argued) fostered "greed," "racism," and "cultural bias" (Espenshade 1992).

In California, often a bellwether state for the rest of the nation, the immigration issue gained particular prominence. During the summer of 1994, Pete Wilson, then Governor of California, sought a second term, but was running behind in the polls. His numbers changed when he added immigration reform to his platform. Among Wilson's tactics was a television advertisement featuring shadowy people creeping across the highway. "They keep coming," a male voice intoned, "two million illegal immigrants coming across the border." The advertisement's rhetoric sounded an alarmist bell, suggesting that unauthorized immigrants were overrunning the state.

That summer, a number of grassroots groups organized and collected enough signatures to place Proposition 187, an initiative titled "Save Our State," on the November ballot (Suro 1999). The proponents of the law were mostly white, middle-class voters who felt threatened by the demographic changes in their state (ibid.). They believed that the numerous ills that had befallen California—increased crime and economic insecurity—were due to the presence of unauthorized immigrants (ibid.). Their sentiments were expressed by Barbara Coe, who in 1992 entered an Orange County social service center and vowed to do something about what she viewed as the U.S. immigration problem:

I walked into this monstrous room full of people, babies
and little children all over the place, and I realized nobody
was speaking English. I was overwhelmed with this feeling:
Where am I? What happened here? Is this still the
United States of America? (ibid.)

Coe became an ardent champion for Proposition 187. Drafted by former
INS officials, the proposition sought to prevent unauthorized immigrants
from receiving social or welfare benefits,[9] ban them from public schools and
universities, and prevent them from receiving publicly-funded non-emergency
health care.

Advocates with the post-IRCA immigrant coalitions in northern and
southern California waged a heated campaign to stop proposition 187. They
organized, recruited new allies, prepared talking points, and engaged the press.
Lawyers prepared for litigation in case the initiative went into effect. Although
the proposition began with an enormous lead in the polls,[10] towards the end
of the campaign, the initiative was polling evenly among likely voters (Martin
1995). The change was probably due to the organizing and coalition-building
among teachers, school boards, hospital administrators, and sheriffs who urged
voters to reject the initiative. They argued that turning children out into the
street and denying immigrants health care would harm everyone.

As the campaign drew to a close, passions intensified on both sides. A week
before the election, approximately ten thousand Latino high school students
took to the streets of Los Angeles to protest the initiative. Their anger was
palpable on their faces and the press covered the throngs as they waved Mexican
flags. Within days, the initiative climbed the polls again, winning handily with
a fifty-nine to forty-one percent vote. Governor Pete Wilson was also easily
re-elected. Within hours, however, immigrant advocates enjoined the measure
in both Northern and Southern California State and Federal courts. Ultimately,
both courts declared the matter unconstitutional and, except for minor
provisions requiring penalties on the use of false documents, the measure
never went into effect.

Proposition 187 had a number of long-term ramifications for civil society.
First, its overwhelming passage generated a new breed of activism on both
sides of the spectrum. Restrictionists multiplied and created a number of

9 Unauthorized immigrants were and continue to be ineligible for cash assistance. Their U.S.
citizen-born children are eligible for benefits.
10 In July 1994, Proposition 187 led among likely voters by 62 to 29 percent (Suro 1999).

grassroots organizations throughout the state. On the other side, Latinos, outraged by the proposition, began to naturalize and register to vote in vast numbers. A political operative in California observed: "Republicans did with the Latino community in about two years what the Democratic Party couldn't do in thirty" (Schneider 1999). But as California slowly shifted its politics, Congress took up the very same issues. Civil society's polarized camps would soon meet on the national stage.

2.4 The 1996 Legislation

Although some in the press noted that the numbers of unauthorized immigrants were not overwhelming, they had been steadily rising (Rayner 1996). In addition, the public was barraged by images of immigrants intercepted on the high seas or crossing the Mexico-U.S. border (Espenshade 1995). In the mid-1990s Congress considered several immigration reform bills due to the sagging economy as well as to public anxieties over the first World Trade Center bombing and other security concerns. In addition, the restrictionist lobby was effectively working with media outlets to paint the picture of an out-of-control immigration system. Grassroots restrictionist organizations had grown considerably and were vociferously expressing their views to Congress. Among the organizations founded in the 1990s was NumbersUSA, an effective lobbying organization that later played a key role in derailing reforms.

In 1994, Representative Lamar Smith (R-TX), the new chair of the House Subcommittee on Immigration after the Republican takeover of the House that year, proposed curbs on both *legal* and unauthorized immigration.[11] In 1995, Senator Alan Simpson (R-WY) introduced two companion bills in the Senate. One dealt with border security, asylum, deportation, and restrictions on public benefits; the other called for cuts in the numbers and categories of legal immigrants. While Congress had considered numerous immigration bills during this period, until then it had not targeted legal immigrants. Senator Simpson later combined his two bills.

These issues challenged and divided pro-immigrant advocates within civil society. In order to protect legal immigration, immigrant advocates in Washington, D.C. built a left-right coalition that framed the debate surrounding legal immigrants as a defense of family (Wong 2006). Joining forces were civil liberty organizations like the ACLU, faith-based groups such as the U.S. Conference of Catholic Bishops (USCCB), ethnic groups like NCLR and the National Asian Pacific American Legal Consortium (NAPALC), and libertarian

---

11 Immigration in the National Interest Act of 1996, H.R. 2202.

and conservative groups such as the Cato Institute, the Alexis de Tocqueville Institution, and Americans for Tax Reform. Arguing that legal immigrants should not be punished for the acts of unauthorized immigrants, they lobbied to split the bill.

The rhetoric over unauthorized immigrants incensed many immigrant advocates and activists outside of Washington, D.C. They believed that unauthorized immigration measures stood more of a chance of defeat if both bills were kept together and they considered the coalition's tactics a betrayal of immigrant communities. National advocates, however, believed otherwise and opted for the more pragmatic strategy. Ultimately, the bills were separated.

In 1996, Congress passed three sweeping bills: the *Anti-Terrorism and Effective Death Penalty Act* (AEDPA),[12] the *Personal Responsibility and Work Opportunity Act* (PRWORA)[13] and the *Illegal Immigration and Immigrant Responsibility Act* (IIRIRA).[14] The legislation dramatically changed the immigration landscape.

President Clinton signed the AEDPA into law on the year anniversary of the Oklahoma City bombing even though the perpetrators in that terrorist attack were not immigrants. The two other laws dealt severe blows to immigrants. IIRIRA instituted mandatory detention, expanded the definition of aggravated felony, barred most immigration remedies, and instituted expedited removal procedures which required summary deportation of individuals arriving at U.S. ports of entry with false or no documents. The PRWORA drastically reduced benefits to legal immigrants and refugees. Additionally, both the IIRIRA and the AEDPA sharply curtailed immigrants' right to judicial review and habeas corpus.

Supported by the Ford Foundation and a number of other foundations, immigration advocates mobilized in response to the legislation. Legal support agencies and bar associations analyzed the legislation and began to educate the field on the new laws. Litigators filed lawsuits contesting some of the most draconian features of the legislation, including those involving expedited

---

12 Pub. L. 104-132, 110 Stat.1214 (April 24, 1996).
13 Pub. L. 104-193 (August 22, 1996).
14 Pub. L. 104-208, 110 Stat. 3009-546 (September 30, 1996).

removal for asylum seekers and those stripping the courts of jurisdiction.[15] Advocates in sympathetic states appealed to their governments to restore some of the most egregious cuts in the safety nets available to immigrants, and Washington, D.C. advocates lobbied Congress to restore some of the benefits (Pear 1997).

In September of 1996, shortly after passage of the legislation, George Soros, a multi-billionaire and Hungarian immigrant who had become a naturalized citizen, announced the creation of a $50 million, three-year fund to help immigrants naturalize and thereby avoid losing public benefits. Soros called the new fund Emma Lazarus and housed it within the Open Society Institute. After decades of decline, the rate of naturalization among the nation's immigrants rose sharply (Johnson et al. 1999). A multi-site program administered by the Catholic Legal Immigration Network, Inc. (CLINIC) alone naturalized 45,000 immigrants who were at risk of losing public benefits.

2.5 Early 2000 and the Possibility of Legalization

By 2000, Congress had restored some of the severest cuts to benefit programs under the 1996 welfare law (Broder 2005). It had also modified protections that Central Americans had lost under the IIRIRA and increased the budget for naturalization. The press noted the changes in tone (Ojito 1998). Additionally, under pressure from regional coalitions such as those in New York and California, some states provided safety nets for immigrants that had been deprived of benefits. An economic boom in the late 1990s helped generate a more relaxed atmosphere.

It was clear by 2000 that some of the severest restrictions had consequences that ran counter to congressional intent. Beefed up patrols at high-volume crossing points led migrants, (and their smugglers), to take more hazardous routes and compelled many unauthorized immigrants to stay in the United States rather than risk not being able to return. Migrant fatalities increased, as did the unauthorized population. Advocates began to call for immigration reform legislation.

---

15 In *INS v. St. Cyr*, 533 U.S. 289 (2001), the Supreme Court ruled that immigrants awaiting deportation under provisions of the 1996 immigration legislation could not be denied their habeas corpus rights to seek release from detention before being summarily deported. In *Zadvydas v. Davis*, 533 U.S. 678 (2001), the Court ruled that immigrants awaiting deportation could not be detained indefinitely if their country of origin refused to admit them.

Conditions for reform seemed to have improved. The business community, which had always supported immigration due to its need for cheap labor, joined with the AFL-CIO, to call for reform. During the IRCA debate, the AFL-CIO supported employer sanctions as a means of curtailing unauthorized immigration and only begrudgingly supported legalization (Burgoon et al. 2010). Over the years, however, the AFL-CIO had grown increasingly supportive of the immigrants' rights agenda and, in February 2000, its executive council passed a resolution denouncing employer sanctions and supporting legalization for all unauthorized workers.

Also in February 2000, the International Migration Policy program at the Carnegie Endowment joined the *Instituto Tecnologico Autónomo de México* (ITAM) to convene a migration panel, bringing together major players in the immigration debate from Mexico and the United States (Carnegie Endowment and ITAM 2001). The bi-national panel issued a set of recommendations just ahead of a February-scheduled meeting between Mexican President Vicente Fox and President Bush, both of whom had recently been inaugurated. The panel began discussing bi-lateral migration policy and outlined a series of core principles that would serve as a guide to comprehensive reform (ibid.). National entities, particularly the Carnegie Endowment, worked on a plan that combined development in sending communities, cooperation on border enforcement, expanded avenues for legal migration, and status for those already in the United States.

Immigration reform had not been a central issue in George W. Bush's campaign for presidency. His platform had included a temporary worker program, additional Border Patrol agents, and dividing the INS into two separate agencies, one for enforcement and another for immigration service (George W. Bush 2000). However, Bush had been the governor of Texas and understood the growing power of the Latino vote. He had aggressively courted Latinos in 2000 and won thirty-five percent of their votes.

During the summer of 2001, the Bush administration entered into negotiations with the Mexican government for a new guest-worker program (Schmidt 2001). The Mexican government proposed a full-fledged "earned legalization" program and under pressure from its own civil society, insisted that such a program contain certain rights for guest workers.

By September 2001, a legalization bill seemed within reach. President Fox visited Washington on September 6, 2001, for an official state visit and in an emotional appeal to a joint session of Congress, requested that the estimated three million unauthorized Mexicans in the United States be granted permanent residence. While President Fox was in Washington, D.C., President Bush raised the possibility that guest workers would be eligible for permanent residency.

Days later, the September 11, 2001, attacks of the World Trade Center occurred. Instantly, all talks of legalization halted. Once again, immigrant advocates found themselves on the defensive, as legitimate security concerns prompted some of the harshest legislation, regulatory schemes, and security tactics in U.S. history. Because the attackers exploited gaps in the U.S immigration system, the government introduced policies to enhance border security, restrict immigration, increase the surveillance of immigrant populations, and more actively enforce immigration law.

2.6 9/11: Security-Related Immigration Restrictions

A few weeks after September 11, 2001, with no public hearings or input, Congress passed the *Uniting and Strengthening America by Providing Appropriate Tools Required to Intercept and Obstruct Terrorism Act* (The USA Patriot Act).[16] The law melded proposals set forth by the Department of Justice and Congressional leaders. Although lawmakers from both parties expressed concerns about the legislation's scope, particularly its impact on civil liberties, every senator and representative, including "immigrant-friendly" lawmakers such as Senators Kennedy and Leahy, voted for the legislation.

The USA Patriot Act included an expanded definition of terrorist, more limits on judicial review, and retroactive application of certain laws. Many of its provisions were slated to sunset in 2005, but the immigration provisions became permanent. In addition to legislation, the government unveiled new policies that affected almost every aspect of immigration law and that went well beyond the 1996 laws (Kerwin 2002).

While the government needed to identify and address potential security threats and was justified in revising its laws and policies in light of the World Trade Center attacks, many of the measures it implemented were overly broad, infringed on civil liberties, and employed racial profiling (NILC 2001). Within weeks of the attacks, for example, over twelve hundred noncitizens, most of them men of Middle-Eastern, Muslim, or South Asian descent, were arrested and detained (Volpp 2002). The majority of them had entered legally and

16 Pub. L. 107-52 (October 26, 2001)

their detentions were based on immigration violations (ibid.). Most were held indefinitely without charge and without the right to contact counsel (ibid.). None of the persons arrested during this time were later identified as engaged in terrorist activity (ibid.).

In addition, US Attorney General Ashcroft used his statutory power to implement programs aimed at investigating men from Middle Eastern and South Asian countries. In November 2001, he announced a plan to interview more than 5,000 men aged eighteen to thirty-three from select countries who had entered the United States as nonimmigrants.[17] The Department of Justice characterized these interviews as consensual and cautioned officials to "avoid mentioning individual criminal exposure, but nevertheless to contact INS in the event of suspected immigration violations." Of the 2,261 men interviewed, twenty were arrested, most for alleged immigration violations and none on charges related to terrorism. The Department of Justice also issued a rule to arrest and deport men from select countries that had been ordered removed as part of a new "absconder" program.

The Department of Justice also created a series of special registration requirements for immigrants from countries the U.S. government deemed to be potential national security threats (Tumlin 2004).[18] One such program entitled the National Security Entry-Exit Registration System (NSEERS) required all male non-citizens from designated countries who were aged 16 and older and were in the United States on student, tourist, or business visas to be fingerprinted, photographed and interviewed. Another required male non-citizens from designated countries to notify the government of any change of address, employment or school within 10 days of the change. Failure to comply with these mandates could result in arrest, detention and deportation. Individuals received notice of these requirements when they first entered the country, but the government subsequently expanded the program to include individuals who were already in the United States (Center for Immigrants' Rights 2012). In 2011, the Obama administration delisted the twenty-five countries and announced that males from those countries no longer needed to

17 Memorandum from John Ashcroft, Attorney General, to All United States Attorneys, All Members of the Anti-terrorism Task Forces, "Interviews Regarding International Terrorism" (November 9, 2001); (Farragher and Cullen 2001).

18 *Registration and Monitoring of Certain Nonimmigrants from Designated Countries*, 67 Fed. Reg. 57,032 (September 6, 2002).

comply with the program. In 2012, the administration removed the compliance requirements (Waslin 2012). The program, however, still exists and could be reactivated.

Compounding many of the federal government's anti-terrorism programs was the secrecy with which it carried out its policies and its insistence that any dissent would be deemed unpatriotic (Eggen and Schmidt 2001). The government warned federal employees that it should only disclose information requested under Freedom of Information Act (FOIA)—a law that permits individuals to obtain documents from the government—after "full and deliberate consideration" of the numerous implications of disclosure. It concluded by stating that if the department decided to "withhold records, in whole or in part, you can be assured that the Department of Justice will defend your decisions unless they lack a sound legal basis or present an unwarranted risk of adverse impact."[19]

Despite the restraints the federal government imposed, members of civil society not only criticized the government but fought hard against its veiled secrecy and programs that they believed impinged on civil liberties. Pro-immigrant advocates, faith-based and ethnic groups, immigration lawyers, and the private bar, repeatedly filed FOIA requests and otherwise challenged government programs. Organizations such as CLINIC and NILC closely monitored and analyzed the government's programs and issued studies and reports. Certain established organizations like the American-Arab Anti-Discrimination Committee (AADC), which was founded in 1980, assumed a higher profile during this period. AADC, for example, appeared regularly in the press and became a co-plaintiff in the first major legal challenge to section 215 of the USA Patriot Act.[20] The law allows undisclosed government access to individual medical, educational, and library records.[21] New organizations and coalitions also emerged, including the Rights Working Group, which consists of more than 330 local, state, and national organizations, aimed at advocating and protecting civil liberties.

19 Memorandum from John Ashcroft, Attorney General, to Heads of All Federal Departments and Agencies, "The Freedom of Information Act"(October 12, 2001).

20 Section 215 has been challenged on the grounds that it allows the government to effect searches without a warrant or showing probable cause, and prohibits those served with an order (to turn over "tangible things") to disclose this fact.

21 *Muslim Community Association of Ann Arbor v. John Ashcroft*, (E.D. Mich.) 03-72913 (2003). The ACLU filed the case and later withdrew it after Congress amended the law to allow counsel as well as judicial oversight.

One lasting effect of the 9/11 attacks was the enactment of the Homeland Security Act, which dismantled the Immigration and Naturalization Service (INS) and collapsed the department's main components into the new Department of Homeland Security (DHS), a cabinet-level department with the primary mission of fighting terrorism and protecting the homeland. Since that time, immigration has been seen through the lens of terrorism and homeland security.

2.7 2004-2007: A Revival of Comprehensive Immigration Reform

In the fall of 2001, Representative Richard Gephardt introduced a legalization bill. Sidetracked by security concerns, however, the bill barely registered within the executive and legislative branches. Members of the Mexican government also contacted the administration to resume talks but received little attention. It was not until January of 2004, when President Bush issued a major speech on immigration, that talk of reform legislation regained traction. Bush urged Congress to pass legislation which would reflect his principles for reform, including strengthened border security and a temporary worker program. Bush did not propose CIR, but provided a substantial opening for future legislation.

In 2005, Senators Kennedy and McCain authored compromise legislation that among other things provided a path to legalization for the unauthorized. That same year, however, Representative James Sensenbrenner (R-WI) introduced the "Border Protection, Anti-Terrorism and Illegal Immigration Control Act" of 2005, H.R. 4437. Among its provisions, the bill called for building a 700-mile border fence and further expanding the definition of aggravated felony to include those who entered or re-entered the country in an unauthorized manner. In addition, under the Sensenbrenner bill, priests, clergy and humanitarians who "assisted" unauthorized immigrants could have been charged with a crime (Jonas 2006).

Following the passage of the bill in the House of Representatives, a number of communities held local demonstrations. In early 2006, after Los Angeles academics and community leaders strategized a response, the number of people attending rallies and mobilizations began to grow and in subsequent marches, the numbers exploded. In early March, an estimated 20,000 to 40,000 immigrants and their supporters marched in Washington, D.C. A few days later, an estimated 100,000 to 300,000 people marched in Chicago. In Dallas, the demonstrations drew between 350,000 and 500,000 people, the largest civil rights marches in that city's history (Associated Press 2006). In Schuyler, Nebraska, a town of 5,300, approximately 3,000 people rallied for immigrant rights (Wang and Winn 2006).

The Catholic Church played a key leadership role in these mobilizations by informing their congregations about the events. Cardinal Roger Mahony drew the ire of some Catholics and others by urging people to engage in civil disobedience if the laws actually passed (Watanabe 2006). The ethnic media, particularly a few Spanish language radio personalities, gave significant play to the mobilizations and were instrumental in publicizing them. New technologies such as text messages and MySpace were also widely used (Melber 2006).

On May 1, 2006, organizers not only planned enormous national demonstrations, but also called for a nationwide economic boycott they termed, "A Day Without Immigrants." Although estimates on the number of attendees are difficult to ascertain, from Los Angeles to Miami, millions marched in over fifty cities (Hamilton 2006). The peaceful demonstrations attracted a diversity of marchers including people of Polish, Irish, Asian, and African descent. While the turnout was high, media observers found it difficult to gauge the economic effect of the boycott. Some employers allowed their workers to attend the march; others kept to business as usual. The press and media covered the marches extensively (Archibold 2006).

Immigrant advocates hoped to harness the strength and power of those mobilizations and translate them into action in Washington, D.C. They wanted a bill that would legalize the growing number of unauthorized immigrants, then estimated at more than twelve million people. However, Congress remained deeply divided that year. The Sensenbrenner bill passed the House, while the Senate passed SB 2611, which provided for increased border security, a temporary worker program, and a legalization program for long-term unauthorized residents that agreed to leave the country to apply. These bills died in the 109th Congress.

In 2007, with the backing of President Bush and a bipartisan group of senators led by Senators Edward Kennedy (D MA) and John Kyl (R-AZ), talks on a comprehensive immigration bill revived (Pear and Rutenberg 2007). The resulting bill provided for increased border security, earned legalization, a temporary worker program, and a points system for visas that would have largely scuttled the family visa program in favor of employment visas for skilled workers. Although a group of senators had coalesced around the bill, it faced opposition from both the left and the right. The restrictionist lobby maintained a steady outcry against legalization while the point system and guest worker provisions were barely palatable to labor and immigrant advocates on the left.

Immigration advocates became deeply divided over the bill. Several Washington insiders, including the National Immigration Forum, wanted to see the bill enacted while others thought that the bill was so flawed it should be defeated. The latter groups could not support the compromises necessary to keep Republicans on the bill (Rosenblum 2011), provisions that included increased enforcement, a weakened legalization program, and the controversial point system. But it was the vociferous opposition of the restrictionist lobby that largely caused its defeat (Baldwin 2008). While the bill was being debated, NumbersUSA orchestrated a stream of more than one million calls and faxes, causing the Congressional switchboard to break down (Ball 2013a). In June 2007, the U.S. Senate rejected the legislation (Gaouette 2007).

The vigorous engagement of civil society on both sides of the immigration debate characterized the legislative period beginning in 2005 and ending in 2007. On one side, NumbersUSA spurred the flow of so many calls and faxes that it overwhelmed the Capitol Hill switchboard. On the other, an estimated five million persons participated in one of the largest mobilizations in U.S. history. With such strongly held views on either side it is not surprising that legalization failed. Civil society had reached a stalemate.

2.7.1 A Backlash and Immigrant Response

Not only did the rallies and marches fail to produce the legalization program for which immigrant rights advocates had hoped, but the stalemate in Congress prompted a backlash. As immigrants rallied in cities throughout the country, membership in the Minutemen, an armed group that patrols the US-Mexico border and reports immigrants to the Border Patrol, began to increase. Among other initiatives, the group led a caravan of protestors to Washington, D.C. Their numbers were not huge, certainly not in comparison with the numbers of immigrants demonstrating, but they were a strident group that, along with allied agencies, made their collective voices heard in Congress and in state legislatures and localities where the immigration debate was rejoined.

In 2007 alone, state legislatures introduced more than 1,500 immigration bills, the vast majority targeting unauthorized immigrants. States and localities actually enacted some 244 bills (Jordan 2008). Hazelton, Pennsylvania was one such municipality. In 2006, the town of 25,000 enacted a law imposing fines on landlords who rented to unauthorized immigrants. The law also revoked the business licenses of employers who hired them and adopted an English-only policy for city government services. The ordinance's architect was Kris Kobach, a conservative law professor from Missouri, who also advised and drafted similar ordinances for numerous cities and towns. Immigrant advocates, including the ACLU Immigrant Rights Project (IRP) and Latino Justice (previously known as the Puerto Rican Legal Defense Fund or PRLDF) filed suit against the municipality, and in July 2007, a federal district judge enjoined the city from implementing the measure. The ruling affected a number of other municipalities that had attempted to pass similar legislation in their jurisdictions. The city of Hazelton appealed to the Third Circuit Court of Appeals (Kotlowitz 2007).

Additional states followed with stringent laws against immigrants in their localities and, in April 2010, Governor Jan Brewer signed SB 1070, a law that accorded the police broad power to detain anyone suspected of being in the country irregularly and that made the failure to carry immigration papers a misdemeanor. Despite calls to boycott Arizona, some state legislators proposed even more extreme laws. Notwithstanding the Fourteenth Amendment's birthright citizenship clause, one Arizona lawmaker introduced legislation to deny citizenship to babies born in Arizona if their parents could not prove legal status. While the state never enacted that law, thirty-one states introduced legislation in 2011 imitating all or part of SB 1070. Five states – Alabama, Georgia, Indiana, South Carolina, and Utah – passed Arizona-styled "copy cat" laws (NILC 2012).

As voiced by restrictionists, the rationale for these laws was to win the immigration battle by attrition—to render it so difficult for unauthorized immigrants that they would pack up and return home (Krikorian 2004). Such a rationale did not take into consideration the complexity of families whose members had "mixed" immigration statuses, the long tenure of many living in the United States, or the economic realities of unauthorized immigrants. The US government filed suit to enjoin SB 1070 and a Federal District Court issued a preliminary injunction preventing four of the state's provisions from taking effect. The Ninth Circuit Court of Appeals affirmed the lower's court's decision and the state of Arizona appealed the case to the Supreme Court.

In June 2012, the Supreme Court issued a decision upholding the lower court decisions as to three of the law's measures, but allowing Section 2(b), the provision authorizing police officers to question people about their immigration status, to go forward. The court held that enjoining the measure was premature as there was no showing that the enforcement scheme violated federal immigration law. Nevertheless, because a coalition of civil rights groups filed another lawsuit with additional legal claims not addressed by the Supreme Court, the law did not go into effect. Many within the immigrant rights community expected a much harsher outcome from the court and thus considered the high court's decision a victory.

While some immigration advocates litigated, others organized local communities. Advocates staged demonstrations and marches throughout Arizona and in some southern states, including Alabama. Among many activities, they mobilized a caravan carrying 200 workers, activists, students, and community workers to Arizona. In solidarity with unauthorized immigrants who might be subject to what were commonly known as "papers, please laws," the bus passengers carried no identification.

Meanwhile, a coalition of litigators also challenged Arizona-style laws enacted in other states. As a result, federal courts enjoined laws in Utah, Indiana, Georgia, Alabama and South Carolina. While these challenges continue, the number of state immigration enforcement or "attrition through enforcement" bills has diminished.

2.7.2 The DREAMers and the Immigrant Rights Movement

If every movement has a youth story, then the immigrant rights movement has the DREAMers, a group of young persons who, by organizing for reform and achieving a step towards their goals with the Deferred Action for Childhood Arrivals (DACA) program, have orchestrated a sea change in the immigrant rights movement.

Senators Dick Durbin (D-IL) and Orrin Hatch (R-UT) first introduced the Development, Relief, and Education for Alien Minors Act (The DREAM Act) on August 2001. The bill was subsequently amended and Senators Durban and Hatch reintroduced it in 2003, 2005, and 2007. Representatives Gutierrez, Cannon, Diaz-Balart and Berman introduced it in the House over the same period and included it in the CIR bills in 2006 and 2007. And, in 2007, Senator Durbin inserted it as an amendment to the 2008 Department of Defense Authorization Bill.

On December 18, 2010, the DREAM Act passed the House, but when it came up for a vote in the Senate, it fell five votes short of the sixty votes needed to defeat a threatened filibuster. The bill would provide legal status and a pathway to citizenship to young people who arrived as children and who meet certain other conditions.

The DREAMer movement had its start in immigrant student support groups. Initially, a group of UCLA students without immigration status formed a group called Improving, Dreams, Equality, Access and Success (IDEAS). The students shared survival tips and assisted each other in navigating the large university. As the group grew, students began organizing conferences, raising funds to assist others to complete their education, and engaging in policy advocacy. Similar groups began to emerge in different parts of the country (Wong et al. 2012).[22]

With NILC assistance in the mid-2000s, the student groups convened and developed an informal coalition of organizers and advocates dedicated to passing the DREAM Act and in-state tuition bills for unauthorized students in different states. When the DREAM Act failed as part of CIR in 2007, unauthorized youth re-evaluated their agenda and began to build a movement to influence the broader immigrant rights agenda.[23]

In December 2008, the group's leaders convened a coalition meeting in Washington, D.C. and founded the United We Dream Network (UWDN), a group consisting of seven immigrant youth organizations. Within a few short years, the network of students developed into the largest immigrant youth-led organization in the country, representing forty-seven organizations from twenty-four states.[24] Membership has since expanded to over 5,000 immigrant youth leaders throughout the country.[25]

By telling their stories and staging creative acts of civil disobedience, the students captured the attention of the press. Students, who for years had lived in fear of deportation and had never disclosed their statuses to their classmates, were now sharing their stories with the press. The stories ran counter to the pervasive narrative that unauthorized immigrants were criminals. Though unauthorized, these students had lived most of their

22 Interview with DREAMer Walter Barrientos,May 24, 2013.
23 Ibid.
24 Ibid.
25 Ibid.

lives in the United States and were American in almost every way. As they organized and received press attention, their strategies grew bolder. They staged sit-ins in Congress and at the headquarters of the Obama campaign. They walked across conservative swaths of the south, stopped traffic, and participated in hunger strikes. They pressured both the Obama administration and Members of Congress.

In April 2012, Senator Marco Rubio, a Florida Republican, announced that he was preparing a new bill that would provide visas to young immigrants (Preston 2012). The students met with him and praised his efforts. Not long afterwards, the students met with White House staff to make the case that the administration should grant them administrative relief. In late May 2012, the group leaders marshaled more than ninety immigration law professors to sign a letter to the president specifying the legal precedents that the administration could evoke for a large-scale program deferring deportations. At the same time, the United We Dream Network announced new protests and planned acts of civil disobedience. The first, which was to be held in Los Angeles on June 15, 2012, did not occur because President Obama announced the creation of the DACA program on that day.

Deferred Action is a form of discretionary relief that US Citizen and Immigration Services (USCIS) has used to allow certain individuals to remain in the country.[26] In June 2012, President Obama announced a special program that would grant deferred action to unauthorized young people who came to the United States as children and were pursuing education or military service, provided they had no criminal background. While it does not provide legal residency, DACA temporarily suspends the deportation of successful applicants and provides them with work authorization. As of August 2013, USCIS had received 589,000 DACA applications, had approved 455,455, and had denied 9,578 (USCIS 2013).

UWDN breathed new life into the immigrant rights movement, and presented a human face for immigration reform that even some restrictionists admired (Preston 2012). Additionally, the DACA program has served as a test run for a future legalization program.

2.8 Civic Engagement

---

26 Deferred action is a discretionary decision based on the recommendation of a District Director and approval of the Regional Commissioner not to prosecute or deport a particular alien. *Johnson v. INS*, 962 F.2d. 574, 579 (7th Cir. 1992).

Another factor that has strongly influenced immigration policy is the strong voter turnout among immigrants during the last presidential election. As was widely reported, President Obama received seventy-one percent of the national Latino vote (Preston and Santos 2012). According to the Center for American Progress, between 2008 and 2012, Latinos went from 9.5 percent of the electorate to eleven percent (Kelley and Garcia 2012). Their votes were particularly important in swing states such as Florida, Colorado, Nevada, and New Mexico that were key to Obama's success in the election. Although the media has not given as much play to the Asian American vote, Asians voted for Obama at even higher rates (seventy-three percent) than Latinos (Mahtesian 2012).

These percentages did not appear in a vacuum or blossom overnight. They were the cumulative effect of years of organizing. After the passage of proposition 187 in 1994, a group of Latino union organizers decided to help Latinos naturalize, register, and vote.[27] They began in neighborhoods such as East Los Angeles and Pico Union and, with each election, continued reaching out to other unions and the faith community.

In 2004, the Service Employees International Union (SEIU) hired an organizer and extended the civic engagement work to Arizona, Florida, Maine, and Illinois. While remaining nonpartisan, they educated Latinos on how to vote and engaged in phone banking, precinct walking, and media efforts to ensure that Latinos registered and voted. By 2006, the massive mobilizations pumped new energy into the registration work with the slogan, "Today we march, tomorrow we vote."

By 2012, SEIU had joined with the National Association of Latino Elected Officials (NALEO), NCIR and others on a national campaign that included the Spanish language media giants, Univision, Telemundo, and Azteca. Together, these groups engaged in highly visible campaigns that included public service announcements, news programs on civic engagements and use of on-air personalities.

The decisive role of Latinos in the presidential election was not a foregone conclusion. In previous elections Latinos had provided substantial support to Republican candidates, including President George W. Bush. Latinos had grown disheartened by President Obama's aggressive deportation program,

27 Telephone Interview with Ben Monterroso, Civic Participation Director for Services Employees International Union (SEIU) (May 24, 2013).

hovering at about 400,000 deportations a year (Lemer 2012). Moreover, as Latino voters are not a single-issue constituency, the president's pro-CIR policies were not conclusive; polls consistently showed that the economy and jobs were (and continue to be) top priorities for Latinos.

Nevertheless, as ninety percent of Latinos report having an immigrant parent or grandparent, immigration is a heartfelt concern in the Latino community (Kelley and Garcia 2012). The Administration's June 15, 2013, announcement to halt deportations of young people rekindled Latino support for Obama, especially when contrasted with Mitt Romney's endorsement of self-deportation strategies and repeal of the DACA program. After the election, the President renewed his commitment to passing reform legislation. However, by the end of 2013, despite considerable advocacy from pro-immigrant civil society, broad immigration reform legislation remained as elusive as it had been for more than a decade.

3. The Sectors: Nongovernmental Organizations (NGOs) Engaged on Behalf of Immigrants

US civil society actors in the immigration field run the ideological, geographic, ethnic, and operational gamut. This section highlights the diversity and reach of civil society by describing the key sectors engaged in immigration policy, advocacy and service-delivery, and the work of select agencies in each of these sectors.

3.1 National Advocacy Organizations

Traditionally, the national immigration organizations housed in Washington, D.C. have coordinated immigration reform discussions and advocacy. Their close proximity to Capitol Hill and access to lawmakers give them the opportunity to work on legislation. These organizations have included a cluster of ethnic, faith-based, and civil rights groups such as the National Council of La Raza (NCLR), United States Conference of Catholic Bishops (USCCB), Asian American Justice Center, Leadership Conference on Civil Rights, Center for Community Change, American Immigration Lawyers Association, and National Immigration Forum.

In 2003, the groups formed the Coalition for Comprehensive Immigration Reform (CCR), a nationwide effort aimed at securing enactment of an immigration overhaul. The coalition broadened its support among business leaders and labor, but after several attempts over many years its efforts fell short. One of the reasons the final bill failed in 2007 was that many pro-CIR groups withdrew their support for it. Consensus withered and the restrictionist lobby weighed in heavily for its defeat.

Its failure spurred finger-pointing, divisiveness, and bitter excoriation, but also soul-searching among the leadership and member groups. The Coalition for Comprehensive Immigration Reform folded, and after much review and evaluation, immigrant rights organizations devised new strategies. These included a greater emphasis on communications, a stronger grassroots network with linkages to the nationwide effort, increased citizenship and civic participation, and a revised policy approach.

In November 2012, a group of eight senators (referred to as the Gang of Eight) began meeting to discuss immigration reform (Kim 2012). The group's members include: Democratic Senators Charles Schumer (NY), Dick Durbin (IL), Michael Bennett (CO), Robert Menendez (NJ), and Republican Senators, John McCain (AZ), Lindsey Graham (SC), Marco Rubio (FL), and Jeff Flake (AZ). On April 16, 2013, the bipartisan group introduced S.744, a broad overhaul of the law that, among other provisions, would provide a lengthy pathway to citizenship for the unauthorized.

Shortly after S. 744's introduction, immigrant rights groups called a press conference to introduce the Alliance for Citizenship (A4C), a new coalition of human rights and labor unions aimed at fair immigration reform (Foley 2013a). The main work of the coalition takes place through a series of tables where national and policy-oriented groups meet to formulate policy, devise strategy, confer about messaging and media, and communicate with organizations outside of Washington, D.C.

Within the Alliance, there are groups that focus on specific issues. For instance, a coalition calling itself the Campaign for an Accountable, Moral and Balanced Immigration Overhaul (CAMBIO) is made up of A4C members formed with the purpose of educating lawmakers and the public on the harsh immigration enforcement and militarization of the border that is already in place (Foley 2013b). Although CAMBIO creates some redundancy, members wanted a specific forum to ensure that border and enforcement issues would not become lost amid the overall goal of gaining legalization.

Through its vast network, members of the A4C, CAMBIO, and others have meticulously analyzed the bill and supplied lawmakers with proposed amendments. Moreover, organizations are using social and digital media to make the latest information available to their constituencies and the public at-large.

The way this bill is being debated differs as well. DREAMers have attended legislative sessions and are bringing their mothers to hearing rooms. They can be seen in their bright blue DREAMer T-shirts walking Congressional halls and occasionally engaging in exchanges with lawmakers such as Marco Rubio. This strategy provides immigrants who have never participated in the legislative process an opportunity to do so (Nevarez 2013).

A number of organizations on the left are not part of A4C and have formed their own coalition that they call the Dignity Campaign (Bacon 2013). They have renounced S. 744 and are advocating against it. They believe that the current bill's ten-year wait for legalization is far too long and that millions will inevitably be ineligible for relief. They also believe that the bill codifies a system to provide cheap and exploitable labor. The Dignity Campaign boasts fifty endorsements from groups in about a dozen states. It is unclear whether this group will have the political muscle to influence the work of A4C or that any of the campaign's goals will find their way to legislative proposals. However, its presence may create space for additional shifts in policy.

Three additional entities—the American Bar Association's (ABA's) Commission on Immigration, the National Immigrant Justice Center (NIJC) in Chicago and Americans for Immigrant Justice (AIJ) in Miami—engage in national and regional advocacy, impact litigation and direct services to vulnerable immigrant populations. Each also produce cutting-edge human rights and legal reform reports, enjoy extensive *pro bono* legal networks, and have been particularly engaged on immigration enforcement issues, including the treatment of immigrant detainees.

3.1.1 National Organizations in Favor of Restricting Immigration

Among the groups that favor fewer immigrants and more stringent enforcement measures are three national organizations based in or near Washington, D.C., the Federation for American Immigration Reform (FAIR), the Center for Immigration Studies (CIS), and NumbersUSA. These groups have roots in the zero-population growth movement and links to John Tanton, a Michigan ophthalmologist considered by some to be the father of the restrictionist movement (Anti-Defamation League 2008). According to the Southern Poverty Law Center (SPLC), which undertook a review of his papers at the Bentley Historical Library at the University of Michigan, Tanton has a record of "fretting about the educability of Latinos and warning whites of being out-bred" (Beirich 2009).

Tanton founded FAIR in 1979 to advocate for reductions in immigrant entries, both legal and unauthorized. Since then, the organization has grown and become well established. Its director has testified numerous times before Congress,[28] has developed strong connections with many conservative lawmakers, and is widely quoted in the press. FAIR is the parent organization to the Immigration Reform Law Institute, which served as the intellectual architect to state attrition through enforcement or self-deportation laws. The group's language tends to be nuanced. However, its director has also reportedly said that immigrant groups were engaged in "competitive breeding aimed at diminishing white power," and has espoused a substantial decrease in the US population (Southern Poverty Law Center 2001). Tanton continues to serve on FAIR's board of advisors.

The Center for Immigration Studies (CIS) is a think tank that generates studies and publications, and has a strong media presence. CIS began as a project of FAIR, where its long-time executive director, Mark Krikorian, previously worked. CIS is more tempered in its rhetoric and evidence-based in its positions than many agencies that advocate to reduce immigration. Like FAIR, it expresses support for substantially reduced legal immigration, greater enforcement of the laws, and fuller integration of the (fewer) immigrants admitted. It has vigorously disputed FAIR's designation as a "hate group" by the SPLC, while also disavowing John Tanton's "big-tent philosophy that embraces some figures who do not play a constructive role in the immigration debate" (Kammer 2010).

NumbersUSA, a group based in Northern Virginia, might best be described as the grass-roots arm of the restrictionist movement. Its director Roy Beck also worked for Tanton as an editor of his newsletter (Ball 2013a). NumbersUSA's main concern is the effect of immigration on the environment and economy. The group boasts hundreds of thousands of grassroots supporters and its media and marketing savvy rival that of some political campaigns. The group has been highly successful at mobilizing its constituents, targeting lawmakers, and influencing media coverage.

---

28 FAIR claims that it has been called to testify on immigration bills before Congress more than any organization in America. (Anti-Defamation League 2008).

All three of the organizations have extensive national networks that participate in town hall meetings, call, write, meet with members of Congress, and advocate passionately against high levels of legal immigration and the presence of unauthorized immigrants in the United States. Like their counterparts in the immigrant rights movement, these groups take full advantage of social media to advance their positions.

3.2 State, Regional and Local Coalitions

Over the last several years, state immigration legislation has mushroomed and local coalitions have responded in turn. In 1996, when Congress cut benefit programs to legal immigrants, a handful of organizations worked to convince their legislatures to fill in the gaps for immigrants in their states. Over time, state groups have had to work defensively to stem the tide of anti-immigrant legislation.

At this writing, at least a dozen coalitions and countless local and regional groups are working on immigration issues in their communities. These groups have proven to be sophisticated, grassroots organizers: they have forged alliances with religious, business, law enforcement, and other unlikely allies to defeat restrictionist legislation. In Florida, for example, the "We Are Florida" campaign organized for a year and mobilized thousands of people to protest and testify against an Arizona-styled law (NILC 2012). A similar coalition defeated immigration enforcement bills in Texas (ibid.). Strong, well-established coalitions also succeeded in passing pro-immigrant state legislation and securing favorable administrative policies. For example, in 2005 the Illinois Coalition for Immigrant and Refugee Rights was instrumental in advocating for the "New Americans Executive Order," a measure establishing a citizen's council comprised of business, faith, labor, philanthropic and community leaders with immigration expertise to help guide immigration policy (Lydersen 2006). Similarly, in 2003, the New York Immigration Coalition lobbied to establish Executive Order 41 (Tung 2009), which provides immigrants with access to all city services regardless of status (NILC 2013).

The immigrant coalitions are able to marshal strength within their own regions, and are also connected with other coalitions as well as to national policy organizations. Through conferences and other mutual work, these local networks have developed interstate relationships that have allowed them to strategize, brainstorm, and share best practices.

In 2013, they achieved significant legislative victories. At the beginning of 2013, only three states, Washington, New Mexico, and Utah, had enacted laws giving unauthorized immigrants access to driver's licenses. By October 2013, eight additional states—Illinois, Maryland, Oregon, Nevada, Colorado, Vermont, Connecticut, California and the Commonwealth of Puerto Rico— had passed legislation to provide unauthorized immigrants with access to driver's licenses. In addition, at least eighteen states now have tuition equity laws or policies, which allow unauthorized residents to pay in-state tuition at community colleges and at some state colleges and universities (ibid.).

Local communities such as Oakland, California and New Haven, Connecticut have passed legislation to make identification cards available to all their residents (Gonzales 2013). These cards have allowed immigrants to open up bank accounts and to avoid having to carry large amounts of cash, thus becoming easy targets of criminals. All these measures have been achieved through the concerted work of state groups in conjunction with national organizations such as the NILC and the ACLU Immigrant Rights Project.

Statewide coalitions have also taken on the broader challenge of immigrant integration. The New York and Illinois Coalitions have established civic engagement programs that assist in naturalizing and mobilizing immigrants to register to vote. They also host an annual nationwide conference to share best practices on ways to draw immigrants into civic life.

Welcoming America is a national, grassroots-driven collaborative that works to promote mutual respect and cooperation between foreign-born and US-born Americans. The program began in 2005 with the Tennessee Immigrant and Refugee Rights Coalition (TIRRC). Tennessee had recently experienced fast demographic changes, incorporating Somali refugees as well as a sizeable Latino population.[29] Prior to TIRRC's welcoming project, tensions between immigrants and native-born residents ran high. Among other incidents, the spouses of immigrants employed at international corporations were harassed, their children bullied, and a mosque was burned down.[30] TIRRC founded "Welcoming Tennessee" in an attempt to address the demographic changes in a constructive way.

Welcoming Tennessee offers tools for new neighbors to engage with each other in a low-pressured, non-politicized way – through cultural events and

29 Interview with Rachel Steinhardt, Deputy Director, Welcoming America, May 16, 2013.
30 Ibid.

potluck meals, for example.[31] Program staff believes that service providers and policymakers have not devoted sufficient attention to receiving communities. Organizers credit their program with diffusing tensions and improving the climate for immigrants in their state. The program has helped to defeat an English-only initiative and other anti-immigrant measures in Tennessee.[32]

The program soon expanded nationally and, through Welcoming America, has become active in twenty-two states (Steinhardt 2013). The program offers tool kits and expert advice on how community members can begin to know and dialogue with each other. It also developed a model resolution with sets of principles and welcoming values that communities can pass in their localities. Rather than attempting to persuade people through public policy discussions, Welcoming America works with receiving communities to acknowledge the social and cultural fears that are stirred when newcomers arrive and their cities and towns begin to change. Ironically, these non-political ice-breakers have successfully toned down extremist, anti-immigrant rhetoric and achieved greater understanding in communities. Welcoming America also works with state immigration coalitions on integration initiatives, with the aim (in part) of creating a climate that is more conducive to immigration reform.

On the other side of the debate, groups that favor greater restrictions and enforcement have created a large contingent of state and local organizations and coalitions with a national reach. Grassroots coalitions and groups have been active in Washington, D.C., Virginia, Maryland, New Jersey, Georgia, Arizona, North Carolina, and California. These groups often coordinate their work with FAIR, NumbersUSA, and the Minutemen (Anti-Defamation League 2008).

After 2010, the number of restrictionist groups began to diminish (Beirich 2013). Their decline appears to be driven by scandals, sniping among groups and co-optation of the movement's goals by state legislatures (ibid.). In 2012, the number of groups plunged eighty-eight percent from their high-water mark of 319 groups in 2010. In 2012, SPLC reported thirty-eight restrictionist organizations (ibid.). At the same time, the restrictionist movement also experienced a noticeable decrease in financial support (Burghart 2012).

The shift has given way to a rise in immigration activism within Tea Party groups (ibid.). One of the Tea Party's six national factions, the 1776 Tea Party,

31 Ibid.
32 Ibid.

recruited its staff leadership directly from the Minutemen. As the Tea Party is larger and stronger than the grassroots restrictionist organizations, the shift could bode well for their cause. On the other hand, the immigration issue could be diluted among a number of other Tea Party causes or associated with Tea Party positions and tactics.

3.2.1 Business and Labor

Business wields tremendous power over government. Industries influence lawmakers in myriad ways, including through campaign contributions and direct lobbying.[33] In fact, high tech and other corporations lobbied and were able to insert many of their proposed fixes into S. 744 (Lizza 2013). Low-skilled worker issues, however, have been the subject of intense negotiations between business and labor.

The first set of talks occurred between the U.S. Chamber of Commerce and the president of the AFL-CIO (ibid.). Labor groups wanted to ensure that guest workers would not be paid less than the median wage in their respective industries. The two sides compromised by agreeing that guest workers would be paid the higher of the prevailing industry wage (as determined by the U.S. Department of Labor) or the actual employer wage (Parker and Greenhouse 2013). Under the agreement, guest workers would also be allowed to pursue a path to citizenship and to change jobs after they arrived in the United States.[34] Another hurdle involved the specific types of jobs that would be included in the guest worker program. Although some low-skilled construction workers would be included in the visa program, construction unions persuaded the negotiators to exclude certain types of skilled jobs such as crane operators and electricians (ibid.) Finally, although business groups wanted 400,000 guest workers, the number of visas granted each year under S. 744 would rise to 200,000 (ibid.).

Senator Feinstein (D-CA) led additional negotiations between the United Farmworkers Union (UFW), the American Farm Bureau and four lawmakers

---

33 Immigration is one public policy area in which large business interests have not regularly prevailed. This may change as more military contractors gain and expand a foothold on the border (Lipton 2013).

34 The National Guestworker Alliance, a project organized to protect temporary workers, believes that although the bill provides for portability (e.g., workers can change employers), in practice finding another employer that is registered within the guestworker program within sixty days will be nearly impossible (Mitchell 2013).

(Silva 2013). In April 2013, agribusiness and labor compromised on a plan that included visas for farmworkers and their families, and a shorter pathway to permanent residency for farmworkers than for other migrants. However, labor had to offer concessions including the creation of a new temporary agricultural program to replace the current H2A program.[35]

Organized labor served as the chief negotiator on behalf of immigrants. Yet, labor, including the UFW, has not always stood alongside unauthorized immigrants. Unions seek higher wages and better working conditions for rank and file members and unauthorized immigrants are often perceived to undercut wages and benefits.

During the 1970s and 1980s, labor support for immigration was mixed. Yet as its immigrant base grew, organized labor's solidarity with immigrants solidified. Despite its prior opposition to day laborers, in 2000 the AFL-CIO publicly endorsed a new amnesty for unauthorized workers and announced its opposition to employer sanctions.

By 2006, organized labor had ratcheted up its support for CIR, including an earned path to citizenship for the unauthorized, as evidenced by a partnership between AFL-CIO and the National Day Laborer Organizing Network, (NDLON) (Rathod 2007). The AFL-CIO/NDLON pact identified shared objectives, such as pursuit of CIR, workplace rights and a path to citizenship for the unauthorized. While the agreement reflects organized labor's shift towards immigrants' rights, it also demonstrates the growing influence of NDLON, a network of more than 140 worker centers spread across thirty-one states. As the immigration debate has unfolded, worker centers have gained recognition for their ability to organize and mobilize immigrant workers, their media savvy, and their advocacy skills.

Another significant player in the labor sector is the National Domestic Worker Alliance (NDWA), a national organization comprised of thirty-nine local membership-based affiliate organizations of over 10,000 nannies and housekeepers located in fourteen states and the District of Columbia. In the 1930s, when Congress enacted worker protections in the National Labor Relations Act (NLRA), it specifically excluded domestic workers and farmworkers. In 2010, after a six-year grassroots campaign, the Governor of New York signed into law the Domestic Worker's Bill of Rights, the first state law to ensure basic labor protections for domestic workers. Later in 2013,

---

35 Interview with Bruce Goldstein, Executive Director, Farmworker Justice, May 16, 2013.

California and Hawaii followed suit (Li 2013; Marinucci 2013). Active drives for similar legislation are pending in Connecticut, Massachusetts, Washington, Illinois, and Oregon (Dean 2013).

3.2.2 Faith-Based Organizations

As noted throughout this paper, the faith-based community has had a long tradition of ministry, direct services, refugee resettlement, and advocacy with immigrants. Some religious institutions, such as the Catholic Church, have long histories that are intertwined with migration and the settlement of immigrants.

The reach and influence of the Catholic Church over immigration policy is quite vast and will soon be extended and tested even further. Catholics constitute the largest single religious denomination in the United States (Jelen 2003). Moreover, this large component of the population is disproportionately concentrated in large, urban, "swing" states rich in electoral votes (ibid.).

In 2003, troubled by deaths of migrants in the Mexican and American deserts, the separation of families, workplace abuses and the growing unauthorized population, the U.S. and Mexican bishops issued a joint pastoral statement entitled, *Strangers No Longer: Together on the Journey of Hope.* Drawing from Scripture and Catholic teaching documents, the statement outlines the bishops' principles for reform, including an earned legalization program (ibid.).

In May 2005, U.S. Catholic bishops launched a national campaign entitled, "Justice for Immigrants, A Journey of Hope." The campaign supports increased economic development in immigrant sending communities and earned legalization for unauthorized immigrants. The campaign also supports expansion of employment- and family-based immigration (Kerwin 2006).

In late August 2013, the USCCB announced a plan to expand the campaign's reach (Parker and Shear 2013). In September 2013, Catholic bishops and priests across the country preached a coordinated message backing changes in immigration policy and urging Congressional passage of legalization for unauthorized immigrants. The campaign included advertising and phone calls directed at sixty Catholic Republican lawmakers and "prayerful marches" in congressional districts where the issue has become a divisive topic (ibid.).

These advocacy efforts came on top of the already substantial work of Catholic institutions with immigrants. For example, the Catholic Church supports large networks of immigrant rights and service agencies through

Catholic Charities USA, the Campaign for Human Development, and the Catholic Legal Immigration Network, Inc. (CLINIC). CLINIC is one of the largest charitable legal service providers and advocacy organizations for immigrants in the nation. Since its founding in 1988, CLINIC's network has grown from seventeen immigration programs to 245 programs that serve immigrants in 350 offices in forty-six states, the District of Columbia, and Puerto Rico. Each year, these agencies provide direct legal and related services to hundreds of thousands of low-wage and vulnerable immigrants. In addition to its direct services, CLINIC provides technical support to state Catholic Conferences on state and local immigration legislation, runs large-scale *pro bono* projects, and advocates extensively with federal immigration agencies. Its parent organization, the USCCB, is deeply steeped in immigration policy at the national level and administers, through its Migration and Refugee Services (MRS) division, the nation's largest refugee resettlement network. MRS has resettled more than one million refugees since 1975.

Catholics also influence immigration policy through entities such as the Scalabrini International Migration Network (SIMN), an umbrella organization established in 2005 by the Congregation of Missionaries of Saint Charles, Scalabrinians. Since 1887, the Scalabrinian Congregation has provided social, legal and religious services to migrants and has advocated for the rights of migrants in immigrant-populous cities throughout the United States. The Congregation contains 250 entities and groups involved in various activities and services helping migrants throughout the world. In addition to its ministries, the SIMN produces cutting-edge scholarship and engages in advocacy before national, regional and international bodies.

Other Christian denominations and churches also exert significant clout over immigration policy. Inspired by the African-American Southern Christian Leadership Conference led by Dr. Martin Luther King Jr., the National Hispanic Christian Leadership Conference (NHCLC) was founded in 2001 to serve Latinos within its 10,700 U.S. churches and exert a collective Latino voice before legislative, economic, and ecclesiastical authorities in Washington, D.C. and in state capitals (Espinosa 2007). The organization is nonprofit and strictly nonpartisan, reaching both liberal and conservative lawmakers.

In 2006, the Reverend Samuel Rodriguez of the NHCLC stated in an interview in the *Washington Post* that the immigration reform debate was a watershed moment between Euro-Americans and Latino Evangelicals. He argued that if Euro-Americans joined the immigration reform movement, they would forge a positive relationship with Latinos that would last for decades, but if they did not, a definitive schism might result (ibid.). During the legislative battles in 2006 and 2007, NHCLC engaged in bipartisan meetings, seminars, and colloquia with key Democratic and Republican political leaders and sought to promote a middle path between the extremes.

During the CIR debate in the 113th Congress, the NHCLC and other Evangelical Churches established an Evangelical Table to meet and strategize on the legislation. Like the Catholic Bishops, they use the biblical text to sway Republicans to support CIR. They are also using traditional advocacy methods such as targeted calls, letter writing, and visits to lawmakers. They hope to gain the support of Republicans from conservative districts whose constituents largely oppose CIR (Davis 2013).

Faith-based groups have been able to reach out to new partners including members of Evangelical churches. As more immigrants have joined their congregations, Evangelical churches have developed more pro-immigrant perspectives. Their support for CIR provides access to conservative members of Congress, particularly those in the House, who have not supported pro-immigrant policies in the past. It is noteworthy that pro-CIR advocates increasingly include groups that are bitter foes on other issues. While faith-based groups can open conservative doors, and are strongly protective of immigrants, they do not support progressive stances such as immigration benefits for same sex marriage partners.

Among other active and well-established faith-based organizations engaged in immigrant work and advocacy are the American Friends Service Committee (AFSC), Hebrew Immigrant Aid Society (HIAS), the Jewish Family and Children's Services (JFCS), the Lutheran Immigration and Refugee Services (LIRS), World Relief Services (WRS), Presbyterian Church USA, and many others.

3.3 Ethnic–Based Groups

Ethnic-based organizations also deliver services to immigrants and participate in developing immigration policy. These entities range from small neighborhood programs to national organizations and umbrella groups such as the Mexican American Legal Defense and Education Fund, the National Council of La Raza, the National Alliance of Latin American and Caribbean Communities, National Asian Justice Center, the Southeast Asian Resource

Action Center (SEARAC), and the American-Arab Anti-Discrimination Committee. Many of these organizations have affiliates throughout the country and are headquartered in Washington, D.C., allowing them access to lawmakers.

An early example of an ethnic organization's involvement in policy change was the American Committee on Italian Migration (ACIM) (Oda 2012). ACIM was established in 1952 with the aim of promoting Italian immigration to the United States. In the fall of 1958, ACIM published a series of letters that expressed the "frustrated hopes" of Italian Americans who wanted to reunite with their families. Over 60,000 such Italians waited for visas with little chance of admission. ACIM began a campaign to enable the immigration of the "fourth preference relatives" of U.S. citizens. These included the married sons and daughters, sons and daughters over age twenty-one, and the brothers and sisters of U.S. citizens. Beginning in 1953, the organization lobbied Congress for legislation that would admit Italians outside the quotas. Through press interviews, radio talks and speaking tours throughout the country, the group brought the plight of separated families to the public's attention. In the years leading up to the final elimination of quotas in 1965, ACIM was successful in obtaining visas for various categories of the excluded family members.

As the above example indicates, the types of issues ethnic organizations become involved in depend on the needs of their constituents. Like the concerns of ACIM, one issue that has surfaced for the Asian American population is that of sibling sponsored petitions. Under current law, immigrant relatives such as parents, spouses, and children of US citizens can immigrate outside numerical limitations. All other relatives such as spouses of permanent residents and adult married children and siblings of U.S. citizens are subject to caps that total 226,000 visas per year. In 2012, fifty-five percent of all Asian immigrants who became permanent residents did so through the family preference categories (Kieu 2013). Yet S. 744 threatens to do away with the sibling category, one of the main pathways for the Asian community. A network of Asian organizations is engaged in advocacy over the issue.

Similarly, for the past eleven years, SEARAC has advocated for reforms against harsh measures under the IIRIRA. These include provisions that expanded the definition of aggravated felonies and eliminated judicial review over relief from deportation for immigrants with past criminal convictions. These changes ensnared an unprecedented number of Southeast Asian youth, who, after serving time for convictions, became subject to new enforcement laws and were automatically detained by INS (now ICE). However, because the United States did not have repatriation agreements with Cambodia, Laos, and Vietnam, the INS detained these individuals indefinitely.

Kim Ho Ma, a Cambodian detainee, challenged his indefinite detention and won his case at the U.S. Supreme Court.[36] After Ma prevailed, the State Department entered into a repatriation agreement with Cambodia, paving the way for deportations of people who had not set foot in their home countries since early childhood. The Southeast Asian community was hard hit by these repatriations. SEARAC has also advocated for reforms to mitigate the harsh enforcement provisions in the 1996 laws, which provide for the removal and mandatory detention of low-level offenders.

Another important organization is the Black Alliance for Just Immigration (BAJI). For decades, restrictionists have attempted to build a wedge between native-born African Americans and immigrants, sounding a constant refrain that immigrants steal jobs from native African Americans. BAJI, a small but growing national organization, has been able to counter such arguments and connect the struggle for immigrant rights with those of civil rights for African-Americans in the south. When Arizona-style state laws began to proliferate in southern states, BAJI stepped up to organize and educate its constituency. BAJI also actively advocates for CIR and works to advance the prospects of immigrants of African and Caribbean descent.

3.4 Hometown Associations

As the name indicates, Hometown Associations (HTAs) are comprised of immigrants from particular towns or regions that wish to preserve their culture, support their communities of origin, and promote their collective interests in the United States (Orozco and Rouse 2007). HTAs from Latin America, the Caribbean and Africa number in the thousands. As these groups mature, they often form nonprofit organizations and expand their goals.

The first formal federation of Mexican HTAs was the Federation of United Mexican Clubs (*Federación de Clubes Mexicanos Unidos*) formed in 1972 by the HTAs from the Mexican State of Zacatecas (ibid.). There are also federations

---

36 The Supreme Court granted certiorari in the *Kim Ho Ma* case and consolidated it with *Zadvydas v. Underdown*, 185 F.3d 279 (5th Cir.1999); it later issued an opinion in the consolidated cases *sub nom. Zadvydas v. Davis*, 533 U.S. 678, 121 S.Ct. 2491, 150 L.Ed.2d 653 (2001).

by destination state such as the federation of Michoacanos Club in Illinois.

An example of a successful HTA that has transitioned into a nonprofit organization is the *Consejo de Federaciones Mexicanas en Norteamérica* (COFEM). COFEM is a membership organization comprised of more than 200 HTAs with over 35,000 active members in Los Angeles, the Inland Empire, the Central Valley and parts of Northern California. In addition to cultural, sports, and social activities, COFEM has become involved in immigration policy and has become very active in naturalization, civic engagement, and get-out-the-vote drives on behalf of Latinos. Like other HTAs, COFEM acts as a bridge between communities of origin and those in the United States.

3.5 Border Organizations

As noted, when the United States government began increasing border enforcement, immigrant smugglers began using different routes. The redirected paths crossed treacherous areas in the Sonoran Desert, resulting in many deaths due to the brutal heat and harsh desert conditions. In October 2003, two faith-based groups began discussing a response. The following year, a group of Catholics and Jews met in Altar, Sonora, Mexico, a staging area for migrants. What emerged was a new organization called "No More Deaths," a local, regional, and national humanitarian organization operating with hundreds of volunteers.

For over ten years, volunteers from No More Deaths have provided water, food, and medical assistance to migrants walking in the Arizona desert. They also monitor the Border Patrol, bring public attention to the plight of migrants, and work towards changing the government's border policy. Together with other nongovernmental groups such as the "Arizona Recovered Human Remains Project," they have successfully publicized a devastating humanitarian problem (Rose 2012).

Not surprisingly, the 2,000-mile long US-Mexican border has been the focal point of what is widely perceived to be the broken immigration system. The United States has spent billions to secure its southern border. In 2012, the U.S. government spent more on its immigration enforcement agencies, nearly $18 billion dollars, than on all its main federal criminal law enforcement agencies combined (FBI, ATF, DEA, Secret Service, and US Marshals), arguably making immigration enforcement the number one law enforcement priority of the federal government (Meissner et al. 2013).

In 2007, the Bush Administration set out to double the Border Patrol. In less than two years, the agency hired 8,000 new agents, to bring its total to 21,000 (Rey 2012). The relatively young and inexperienced force was equipped with batons, pepper spray, Tasers, rifles and handguns and new technology including night sensors, unmanned drones and Black Hawk helicopters (ibid.). Several recent studies of deportees have documented pervasive verbal and physical abuse by Border Patrol agents against migrants (Kerwin 2013). In addition, since January 2010, there have been at least fifteen deaths at the hands of Border Patrol agents in the Southwest (Santos 2013). Most recently, agents fired upon and killed Jose Antonio Elena Rodriguez, a sixteen-year-old boy, who allegedly hurled rocks at them from the Mexican side of the border near Nogales (ibid.).

The debate over CIR has made border security a prerequisite for legalization. S. 744 establishes a goal of achieving a ninety percent success rate in intercepting or turning back unauthorized immigrants who attempt to cross the border.[37]   The Senate approved an amendment by Republican Senators Bob Corker (R-TN) and John Hoeven (R-ND) to set aside more than $46 billion to double the number of border patrol agents along the southwestern U.S. boundary, add new surveillance technology, and complete the 700-mile border fence (Kim 2013). The bill would also increase the number of Customs officers by 3,500 people by 2017, authorize the National Guard to participate in missions related to border security, and fund additional surveillance technology (ibid.).

Under siege for several decades, border communities have been organizing and training themselves, documenting abuses, and advocating for humane and responsible law enforcement. With support from the American Friends Service Committee, the Border Rights Coalition was founded in the early 1990s. A highlight of its work was a landmark 1992 federal class action lawsuit that enjoined the Border Patrol from harassing students and staff from Bowie High School.[38] In 2000, the organization became the Border Network for Human Rights (BNHR).

BNHR works with elected officials, law enforcement agents, academics, faith leaders and others to bring the perspectives of border communities to federal and state policymaking. BNHR has organized border tours for congressional staff and has taken community members to Congress to lobby for humane

37 SBS. 744, Title I, Section 3(a) (3).
38 *Muriillo v. Musegades*, 809 F. Supp. 487 (1992).

enforcement. It has also formed coalitions with other border organizations such as the Southern Border Communities Coalition and CAMBIO. Together they have pressed for border enforcement that is more accountable to affected communities. Among other provisions, BNHR supports: the use of lapel cameras for border agents to ensure that encounters with the public are properly documented; greater authority for the DHS Border Oversight Task Force to ensure adequate accountability; the equal application of constitutional protections to border residents; and the allocation of additional personnel to support business and personal travelers along the border.

Like other members of CAMBIO, border coalitions are working on strategic messaging to create narratives that are better understood in the general public. They have moved from talking about the militarization of the border to discussions of border families and communities that are affected by enforcement policies.[39] Ironically, as CAMBIO members began toning down their rhetoric, members of Congress increased their use of the language of militarization.

On the other side of the political spectrum are a number of groups, organizations, and coalitions seeking even tighter controls on the border. Despite the fact that border crossings have abated significantly[40] and billions of government dollars have been spent on surveillance, technology and beefed up patrols, these groups believe the government is not doing enough to secure the border. These organizations include the San Diegans for Secure Border Coalition, the Texas Border Coalition, the Secure Border Coalition and the Minutemen.

The Minutemen organization had its start in 2005 and received national attention for its armed civilian border patrols of the U.S. southern border (Beirich 2013). Not only was the group patrolling the borders, but its members were also engaged in protesting legislation, writing letters, and videotaping day laborer sites. The number of Minutemen chapters grew significantly after 2006 when the SPLC documented 144 such groups. By 2010, the movement hit a high of 319 groups. Its leader Chris Simcox testified before Congress and together with co-founder Jim Gilchrist made numerous media appearances.

---

39 Interview with Christian Ramirez, Director of Southern Border Communities Coalition, July 24, 2013.
40 According to federal officials, the U.S.-Mexican border that runs along Arizona has seen the lowest number of illegal crossings in twenty years (Huffington Post 2013).

The Minutemen is a group of civil defense volunteers, most of them white, middle-class males who are military veterans. Although the SPLC has documented some violence by groups members—which has diminished the capacity of the movement[41]—the majority of the Minutemen simply patrol border areas and inform the Border Patrol when they spot unauthorized individuals attempting to cross the border, which, according to reports, is very rare (Shapira 2013). By 2011, the Minutemen organizations and chapters had declined to thirty-eight groups and one of the cofounders, Jim Gilchrist, reportedly shifted his energies to the Tea Party.

3.6 Organizations Working on Behalf of Women and Children's Issues

Several organizations advocate on behalf of refugee and immigrant children in the United States. Kids in Need of Defense (KIND), for example, arranges *pro bono* representation for unaccompanied immigrant children throughout the United States. The Migrant Rights and Justice program of the Women's Refugee Commission advocates on behalf of immigrant families that are negatively impacted by U.S. enforcement policies and on issues affecting the well-being of unaccompanied minors. The ABA's Commission on Immigration has also been actively engaged on these issues from an advocacy and direct services perspective.

Two additional groups also stand out for their advocacy efforts. The first is ASISTA, a relatively new organization that grew out of the National Network to End Violence Against Women (the Network). During the 1990s, at a time when the anti-immigrant movement swelled to a boil in California and the rest of the country, this small coalition worked to insert protections for immigrant women into the Violence Against Women Act (VAWA).[42] Through grassroots organizing, the coalition learned that the incidence of domestic violence among immigrants was particularly high.[43] They also learned that batterers used

41 In 2011, Shawna Forde, a leader in the Minutemen Project, was convicted and sentenced to death for murdering a ten-year-old Latina girl and her father (Medrano 2011). In addition, Chris Simcox, one of the co-founders of the Minutemen was charged with sexual molestation of three minor girls.

42 VAWA was passed as Title IV, sections 40001-40703 of the Violent Crime Control and Law Enforcement Act of 1994, H.R. 3355. (P.L. 103-322).

43 Out of 400 immigrant women surveyed in the San Francisco Bay Area, approximately twenty percent reported incidents of violence either in their home countries or in the United States (Lang and Marin 1995).

immigration status as a tool to keep women in precarious situations. If the batterer filed an application to legalize the immigrant spouse and she reported abuse to the police, the batterer would call the INS and withdraw his petition.

The Network formed alliances with women's organizations and those that specifically dealt with family violence such as the Family Violence Prevention Fund (now Futures Without Violence). A Network-drafted provision allowing battered women to self-petition for their immigration status was inserted into the Violence Against Women Act (VAWA), a larger bill that mandated the investigation and prosecution of violent crimes against women. [44] In lobbying for the bill, coalition members downplayed immigrant status and focused on the need for law enforcement against crimes of violence. The bill survived with the immigration provisions intact. It has been subsequently amended several times. Over time, sheriffs and non-immigrant women's organizations have become champions for immigrant survivors of domestic violence and spokespersons on their behalf. Advocates against domestic violence continue their work within the CIR debate.

Like ASISTA, the Center for Gender and Refugee Studies (CGRS) has worked to secure the rights of women, children, LGBTQI individuals, and others who flee persecution in their home countries. Housed at the University of California (UC) Hastings Law School, CGRS provides legal training and mentoring, engages in impact litigation, policy development, research, and uses international human rights tools to advance refugees' human rights and address the root causes of their persecution. Like many other organizations in the immigrant rights field, CGRS is also working in coalition with other experts across the country to remedy some of the most egregious measures in the 1996 laws.

3.7 Think Tanks and Academic Centers

The integrity of the immigration policy debate depends on the contributions by institutions that produce scholarship, research, and evidence-based policy proposals. These organizations educate policymakers, other stakeholders, and the public at large about the needs and challenges facing immigrants and host communities, as well as the consequences of different policy options. For instance, many argue that immigrants act as a drain on public services. However, a May 2013 study by Harvard Medical School measured immigrants' contributions to the part of Medicare that pays for hospital care, a trust fund

44 Interview with Gail Pendleton, Co-Director of ASISTA, June 4, 2013.

that accounts for nearly half of the federal program's revenue. It found that immigrants generated surpluses totaling $115 billion from 2002 to 2009 while the American-born population incurred a deficit of $28 billion over the same period (Tavernise 2013).

Over the years, as the immigration issue has gained more prominence, the number of institutions studying it has also expanded. These include entities with a particular focus on immigration such as the Center for Migration Studies of New York (CMS), the Migration Policy Institute (MPI) and the Center for Immigration Studies (CIS), but they also include institutions like the Brookings Institute, Council on Foreign Relations, Center for American Progress, Cato Institute and the Heritage Foundation which have all made immigration one of their priority issues.

All of these entities tout their nonprofit, nonpartisan identities. However, many of them have distinct political and philosophical bearings. The Cato Institute, for instance, is rooted in libertarian traditions, while the Brookings Institute and the Center for American Progress lean more to the left. CMS works closely with Catholic and other faith-based institutions on international migration issues, and has a "human security" orientation. In its publication, *International Migration Review*, CMS offers scholarly articles and research on migration flows and policies throughout the world.

University centers have also focused on immigration. Like think-tanks, they produce studies from a variety of disciplines including law, political science, sociology, ethnic studies, and history. Georgetown University's Institute for the Study of International Migration (ISIM), for example, regularly generates scholarship, policy analysis, testimony, and events in national and international fora. It also offers a certificate program in international migration. The University of California (UC) Riverside and Davis, the Warren Institute housed at UC Berkeley, and the labor centers at both UCLA and UC Berkeley have contributed significant scholarship on immigration. The Center for U.S.-Mexican Studies based at the University of California in San Diego is one of the oldest academic institutions to study migration policies. It was founded in 1979.

The Transactional Records Access Clearinghouse (TRAC) housed at Syracuse University analyzes government data, including on immigration. TRAC's statisticians are experts at using the Freedom of Information Act in order to collect data and determine whether the government is accomplishing its stated goals. TRAC's analyses of U.S. immigration-related criminal prosecutions, delays in the adjudication of removal cases, and border enforcement practices are widely relied upon by scholars, researchers, government agencies, and NGOs.

3.8 Philanthropy

The growth of the immigrant rights field since IRCA is due in part to the sustained support of the foundation community. The Ford Foundation, for example, first supported the National Immigration Forum in 1981 and funded regional coalitions after the passage of IRCA. Its long-term vision drew in other foundations to sustain a rapidly growing movement. Among the other seminal grantmakers in the field are the Carnegie Corporation of New York, the Open Society Foundations (OSF) and the Rosenberg Foundation.

The philanthropic community has funded a multi-pronged approach to immigrant rights and integration that includes research, communications, public education, litigation, advocacy, community organizing, capacity-building, and networking. Linkages have occurred through conferences, regional meetings, and advocacy and service delivery initiatives. In short, the foundations helped to create a movement. By the 1990s as the nation weathered a maelstrom of anti-immigrant sentiment, state and local coalitions and immigrant-led community organizations responded aggressively. After Congress enacted draconian, immigration-related laws in 1996, the field grew further.

In 1990, Ford and a small group of funders including the Mertz-Gilmore Foundation, the Rosenberg Foundation, the New York Community Trust, and the James Irvine Foundation, joined together to begin an affinity group on immigration. The group became known as Grantmakers Concerned with Immigrants and Refugees (GCIR). What began as a volunteer effort grew quickly: the organization now supports a network of funders from over half of the states in the union. GCIR convenes funders for discussion of pressing issues, offers them technical support, and provides materials on best practices, including to funders that are new to the field (Freedberg and Wang 2008). Foundations, in turn, use GCIR as a forum to coordinate their work and to strategize on how to build the immigrant rights field.

An example of how funders and community-based organizations are working together is the work of the New Americans Campaign (NAC). NAC is a $4 million project funded by Carnegie Corporation of New York (a pioneer and leader on citizenship and immigrant integration), the John S. and James L. Knight Foundation, the Grove Foundation, and the Evelyn and Walter Haas, Jr. Fund. The collaborative brings together national and community organizations to encourage and assist eligible permanent residents to naturalize. A collaborative of funders is also involved in a similar civic engagement project in California.

3.9 Communications and Media Organizations

One of the lessons gleaned from the failure of the 2007 legislation was that the immigrant rights field needed more effective communications capacity. Because opponents of CIR were more successful in conveying their message, the predominant narrative was that unauthorized immigrants were criminals who were stealing jobs from native workers and draining public coffers. Restrictionist groups successfully conflated immigrants with lawbreakers, and portrayed them as a risk to the United States. In response, pro-immigrant advocates have developed new strategies, messages and organizations to address this challenge.

Established in 2008, America's Voice is one such organization. America's Voice's mission is to create a communications war room, an integrated hub aimed at winning broad immigration reform. America's Voice follows the developments of CIR closely, engages with the press and media, and uses all forms of digital media to disseminate its message to the field.

Another media-related organization that works closely with the immigrant rights field is the Opportunity Agenda. Launched in 2004 with the mission of changing hearts and minds to expand opportunities in America, Opportunity Agenda uses communications and media to understand and influence public opinion. It works with social justice groups, leaders, and movements and has targeted immigration policy as one of its key concerns. To that end, Opportunity Agenda has lent its expertise and assisted advocates to communicate their messages more effectively.

In 2010, Opportunity Agenda partnered with the California Immigrant Policy Center (CIPC), a California-based coalition, and commissioned Lake Research Partners of Washington, D.C. to conduct qualitative and quantitative research on immigrant enforcement (Siegel 2012). After analyzing the data, Opportunity Agenda found that advocates were unwittingly referring to immigrants as victims and as people who needed to be helped rather than as hardworking members of communities. Focusing on paths to legalization drew attention to the fact that immigrants were irregularly present, feeding into the frame that restrictionists were already using. Opportunity Agenda made a number of recommendations to the field to ensure better messaging.

Another new media-oriented organization is Define American, a group founded by Jose Antonio Vargas, a Pulitzer Prize-winning journalist. In 2011, Vargas publically revealed his unauthorized status in an essay published in the *New York Times Magazine* (Vargas 2011). Within weeks, the article went viral and attracted worldwide coverage. He then capitalized on the personal publicity he received and created a website and an organization that attempts to put a human face on the more than eleven million U.S. residents without immigration status. The faces and the stories represented on the website are far broader than the stereotype of Mexican males often depicted in the media. They include professional young people from all walks of life, as well as the allies who have assisted them.

In 2012, Vargas was invited to be on the front cover of *Time Magazine* (Vargas 2012). At his insistence, the magazine brought in unauthorized young people to stand beside him. Because of his media background, Vargas has continued to engage the press, pundits, and influential decision makers. In 2013, he testified before Congress and later released a film titled *Undocumented,* which tells his personal story and places it in the context of the struggle for CIR. Mr. Vargas is using the film to spur more discussion over the need for legalization and is inviting influential community and business leaders such as Mark Zuckerberg, the founder of Facebook, to join him (Marinucci 2013).

In addition to these new organizations, established groups have also developed more sophisticated communication strategies. National organizations have made communications a significant priority and have used the media in states such as Alabama and national campaigns. They are paying greater attention to messaging, feeding stories to journalists, and training immigrants to speak directly to the press on their experiences, thus strongly conveying and positioning pro-immigrant messages.

On the other side of the spectrum, immigration restrictionists have enjoyed the support of a number of television and radio personalities championing their cause. Among the most prominent is Lou Dobbs. Dobbs anchored CNN's *Lou Dobbs Tonight* and became well-known for angry, sensationalistic rants against the unauthorized, referring to them, for example, as "illegal aliens who flood across our borders in some cases carrying dangerous diseases" (Hart 2004). Dobbs regularly featured leaders from FAIR and other restrictionist, as well as nativist groups on his show.

In November 2009, after significant protest from Latino advocacy groups, Dobbs announced his departure from the CNN network. He insisted that his exit was not related to protests against him. As the host of the Fox Business Network, he continues to talk about immigration, but has toned down his earlier rhetoric.

In addition to Dobbs, a number of other local and regional television and radio personalities also regularly feature restrictionist leaders and espouse anti-immigrant rhetoric. Among them are Lynn Woolley, a Texas radio personality, and John Kobylt and Kenneth Robertson Chiampou, two radio personalities that host the John and Ken Show out of KFI AM 640 in Los Angeles. In September 2011, "John and Ken" broadcast the phone number of an immigrant rights activist who was working as a spokesperson for the Coalition for Humane Immigrant Rights of Los Angeles (CHIRLA). The activist was championing state tuition assistance for unauthorized immigrant students and the radio hosts urged listeners who opposed the measure to call the activist on his cell phone. The activist was inundated with hate calls (Wilson 2011). The National Hispanic Media Center, a nonprofit media advocacy group on behalf of Latinos, joined forces with NILC and NALEO, and began a campaign calling for an economic boycott of the John and Ken Show. The coalition succeeded in convincing a number of prominent advertisers such as General Motors to cancel their advertising on their show.

Conclusions on the Way Civil Society Is Shaping Immigration Policy

The foregoing has illustrated that the United States has a diverse, vibrant, and expansive civil society that is engaged in immigration policy, advocacy and service-delivery. U.S. civil society consists of impassioned actors on both sides of the immigration debate. This is as it should be: the democratic process itself is messy and the immigration issue is of vital importance. The debate goes to the very heart of American identity as well as the bedrock values emblazoned on the Statue of Liberty. It concerns issues that the United States has struggled over—with various degrees of success and rancor—since its founding. The difference today is that civil society has the ability to communicate widely and immediately. As a result, both immigrant advocates and restrictionists claim millions of grassroots supporters. But just because the United States has a vital and engaged civil society does not mean it will be successful in resolving the situation of the eleven million U.S. unauthorized residents.

The problem could be solved in one of three ways: the government could deport the eleven million unauthorized immigrants (either directly or by "attrition"), could legalize some number of them, or could pursue the status quo. The first solution would be untenable to most Americans since it would require tactics more fitting for a police state and would carry a very expensive price tag. The second would be unacceptable to the restrictionists who have maintained a steady outcry against legalization for several decades. The third is viewed as untenable by actors on both sides of the immigration divide. Pro-immigrant civil society groups have helped to craft a compromise law (S. 744) that reflects the diverse, multiple interests of those groups that favor broad reform. Is this the solution for which the American populace—and their elected representatives—have been waiting? Or will the issue remain mired in the stalemate that has persisted for more than ten years?

Polling shows that a substantial majority of Americans support CIR. Perhaps because pro-CIR advocates have battled restrictionist legislation for so long, they have developed and fine-tuned their strategies. Many of their tactics focus on communications and messaging that resonates with the public, particularly those who occupy the middle. They have employed media consultants and have taught immigrant spokespeople how better to present themselves and their messages. DREAMer activists have provided fresh, new voices that have poignantly amplified the struggle for CIR.

At the same time, restrictionists appear to have lost grounding. According to the SPLC, for two years, the number of hard-line restrictionists groups has fallen. During the August 2013 congressional recess, while immigrant advocates diligently visited lawmakers, staged demonstrations, and held prayer vigils, opponents of CIR were not as visible and their town hall meetings were not well attended (Ball 2013b). In August 2013, a heavily publicized rally opposing "amnesty" in Richmond, Virginia, had a showing of a few dozen attendees, far short of the hundreds of organizers they had expected (ibid.). Moreover, some restrictionist messages, such as those of Steven King, the Republican congressman who claimed most unauthorized youth are drug mules, have fallen flat and have been quickly disavowed by the House speaker John Boehner and by other conservative congressional leaders (Berman 2013).

But even if immigrant advocates are successful in advancing their message, they still have the more arduous task: it is always easier to defeat potential legislation than to build consensus around a bill and negotiate its passage. Nevertheless, there are signs that society is changing in ways that are creating a climate more conducive to legalization. Latinos, the nation's largest and fastest growing minority group, have shown considerable voting power and passion on immigration.

One of the ways demographic and electoral changes are already being felt is in the number of measures that have been enacted on behalf of immigrants at state and local levels. At the beginning of the 2013 legislative session, three states were issuing driver's licenses or driving privilege cards to immigrants regardless of their immigration status. During the year, eight additional states and the Commonwealth of Puerto Rico enacted laws expanding immigrants' access to driver's licenses (NILC 2013). Additional measures have provided tuition equity for immigrant students, rights for domestic workers (the majority of whom are immigrants), and identification cards for immigrants. Thus, while Congress continues to debate CIR, certain states and localities are opting to enact legislation to ease the day-to-day lives of immigrants.

Finally, another change is quietly and incrementally taking place at a state and local level: coalitions of groups have stepped up their naturalization programs and are preparing large numbers of immigrants to naturalize and vote. At the same time, faith communities and groups like Welcoming America are working to diffuse tensions between newcomers and the native born in communities throughout the country. Those changes are not necessarily seen in legislative voting tallies, but in churches, synagogues, schools, workplaces, potlucks, little league games, supermarkets and PTA meetings—places were ordinary people, both immigrant and native-born, meet and work.

These shifts point to an acceptance and readiness for larger-scale changes. What legislation might result and whether Congress in its current polarized, partisan state will be capable of enacting reform in the near-term remains to be seen. What is certain is that civil society is more robust than it has ever been, will remain active in the immigration debate, and will be ready for reform if and when it comes.

Acknowledgements

The author wishes to thank Richard Boswell, Kevin Johnson and Donald Kerwin for their ideas, direction, and careful review of this chapter.

References

Anti-Defamation League. 2008. "Immigrants Targeted: Extremist Rhetoric Moves into the Mainstream." http://archive.adl.org/civil_rights/anti_immigrant/fair.html#. UtDBpvRDt8E.

Archibold, Randall C. 2006. "Immigrants Take to U.S. Streets in Show of Strength." *New York Times,* May 2.

Associated Press. 2006. "'We came, we made history': Hundreds of Thousands March to Support Illegal Immigrant Rights," April 10.

Bacon, David. 2012. "The Modern Immigrant Rights Movement." *Americas Program*, January 14. http://www.cipamericas.org/archives/6080.

———. 2013. "The Dignity Campaign's Alternative Vision for Immigration Reform." *The Nation,* February 6.

Baker, Susan Gonzalez. 1997. "The Amnesty Aftermath: Current Policy Issues Stemming From The Legalization Programs of the 1986 Immigration Reform and Control Act." *International Migration Review* 31(1): 5-27.

Baldwin, Joyce. 2008. "Immigration: The Reform Movement Rebuilds," *Carnegie Reporter.* New York, NY: Carnegie Corporation of New York.

Ball, Molly. 2013a. "The Little Group Behind the Big Fight to Stop Immigration Reform." *The Atlantic,* August 1.

———. 2013b. "Immigration Reformers are Winning August." *The Atlantic,* August.

Banulescu-Bogdan, Natalia. 2011. "The Role of Civil Society in EU Migration Policy: Perspectives on the European Union's Engagement in its Neighborhood." Washington, D.C.: Migration Policy Institute.

Beirich, Heidi. 2013. "The Year in Nativism." Southern Poverty Law Center *Intelligence Report* 149.

———. 2009. "John Tanton and the Nativist Movement." Montgomery, AL: Southern Poverty Law Center. http://www.splcenter.org/publications/the-nativist-lobby-three-faces-of-intolerance/john-tanton-and-the-nativist-movement.

Bennett, Brian, Hector Becerra, and David Lauter. 2012. "Latino Role in Election to Fuel New Immigration Reform Push." *Los Angeles Times*, November, 7.

Berman, Russell. 2013. "Boehner, Cantor Blast Representative Steven King for Drug Mule Comments." *The Hill*, July 24.

Bernstein, Richard. 1993. "Inspector Testifies She Urged No Asylum for Blast Suspect." *New York Times,* November 16.

Blum, Carolyn P. 1991. "The Settlement of *American Baptist Churches v. Thornburgh:* Landmark Victory for Central American Asylum Seekers." *International Law Journal of Refugee Law* 3(2): 347-356.

Broder, Tanya, 2005. "Immigrant Eligibility for Public Benefits." *Immigration and Nationality Law Handbook 759*, 2005-06 ed. Tanya Broder updated the original article written by Charles Wheeler with contributions by Josh Bernstein and Tanya Broder. Washington, D.C.: American Immigration Lawyers Association. http://www.nilc.org/document.html?id=29

Burghart, Devin, and Leonard Zeskind. 2012. "Beyond Fair. The Decline of the Established Anti-Immigrant Organizations and The Rise of Tea Party Nativism." Kansas City, MO: Institute for Research & Education on Human Rights. http://www.irehr.org/images/pdf/BeyondFAIRreport.pdf.

Burgoon, Brian, Janice Fine, Wade Jacoby, Daniel Tichenor. 2010. "Immigration and the Transformation of American Unionism." *International Migration Review* 44(4): 933-973.

Carnegie Endowment for International Peace and ITAM (Instituto Tecnológico Autónomo de México) 2001. "Mexico-U.S. Migration: A Shared Responsibility." Washington, D.C.: Carnegie Endowment for International Peace. http://carnegieendowment.org/pdf/files/M%20exicoReport2001.pdf.

Chishti, Muzaffar, Doris Meissner and Claire Bergeron. 2011. "At Its 25th Anniversary, IRCA's Legacy Lives On." Washington, D.C.: Migration Policy Institute.

Clad, James. 1994. "Slowing the Wave." *Foreign Policy* 95(4): 139-150.

Cohen, Jean L. and Andrew Arato, 1992. *Civil Society and Political Theory.* Cambridge, MA: MIT Press.

Conover, Ted. 1993. "The United States of Asylum." *New York Times Magazine,* September 19.

Curtis, Gregory. 1993. "Guest Editorial: Immigration: R.I.P.? " *Population and Environment* 14 (6): 495-502.

Davis, Julie Hirschfeld. 2013. "Evangelicals Use Bible to Sway Republicans on Immigration." *Bloomberg,* March 6.

Dean, Amy. 2013. "How Domestic Workers Won Their Rights: Five Big Lessons." *Yes!,* October 9.

Eggen, Dan, and Susan Schmidt. 2001. "Count of Released Detainees is Hard to Pin Down." *Washington Post,* November 6.

Espenshade, Thomas Espenshade. 1992. "Policy Influences on Unauthorized Immigration to the United States." *Proceedings of the American Philosophical Society* 136(2): 188-207.

———. 1995. "Unauthorized Immigration to the United States." *Annual Review of Sociology* 21: 195-216.

Espinosa, Gaston. 2007. "'Today We Act, Tomorrow We Vote': Latino Religions, Politics, and Activism in Contemporary U.S. Civil Society." *Annals of the American Academy of Political and Social Science* 612(1): 152-171.

Farragher, Thomas, and Kevin Cullen. 2001. "Plan to Question 5,000 Raises Issue of Profiling." *Boston Globe,* November 11.

Fix, Michael. 1991. "The Paper Curtain: Employer Sanctions' Implementation, Impact and Reform," Santa Monica, CA: RAND Corporation.

Foley, Elise. 2013a. "Citizenship Campaign Launches to Push for Swift

Immigration." *Huffington Post*, February 19.

———. 2013b. "CAMBIO Immigration Coalition Formed to Fight Amnesty Claims." *Huffington Post,* April 12.

Freedberg, Louis and Ted Wang. 2008. "The Role of Philanthropy in the U.S. Immigrant Rights Movement." Unpublished manuscript.

Fuchs, Lawrence. 1993. "An Agenda for Tomorrow: Immigration Policy and Ethnic Policies." *Annals of the American Academy of Political and Social Sciences* 530: 171-186.

Gaouette, Nicole. 2007. "Bill Fails in Senate." *Los Angeles Times*, June 29.

George W. Bush. 2000. "On the Issues: Immigration." http://www.4president.org/issues/bush2000/bush2000immigration. htm.

Gonzalez, Josie. 1993. "Perspectives on Zoe Baird: Blame Congress, INS for 'Wink and Nod.'" *Los Angeles Times*, January 22.

Gonzales, Richard. 2013. "Oakland to Issue I.D.s that Double as Debit Cards." NPR, February 25.

Gzesh, Susan. 2006. "Central Americans and Asylum Policy in the Reagan Era." Washington, D.C.: Migration Policy Institute.

Hamilton, Anita. 2006. "A Day Without Immigrants, Making a Statement." *Time Magazine,* May 1.

Hart, Peter. 2004. "Dobbs Choice." *Fairness and Accuracy in Reporting*, February 1.

Huffingon Post. 2013. "Arizona Illegal Border Crossings at a 20-year Low." February 2.

Immigration and Refugee Board of Canada.1992. "Impact of the September 1991 Coup." http://www.refworld.org/docid/3ae6a81018.html.

Jang, Deeana, and Leni Marin. 1995. "Immigrant Women's Rights Organizing." *In From Basic Needs to Basic Rights*: Women's Claim to Human Rights, edited by Margaret Schuler. Washington, D.C.: Washington Women, Law and Development International.

Jelen, Ted. G. 2003. "Catholic Priests and the Political Order: The Political Behavior of Catholic Priests." *Journal for the Scientific Study of Religion* 42(4): 591-604.

Johnson, Hans P., Belinda I. Reyes, Laura Mameesh and Elisa Barbour. 1999. "Taking the Oath: An Analysis of Naturalization in California and the United States." San Francisco, CA: Public Policy Institute of California. http://www.ppic.org/content/pubs/report/R_999HJR.pdf.

Jonas, Susanne. 2006. "Reflections on the Great Immigration Battle of 2006 and the Future of the Americas." *Social Justice* 33(1): 6-20.

Jordan, Miriam. 2008. "Arizona Seizes Spotlight in U.S. Immigration." *Wall Street Journal,* February 1.

Kammer, Jerry. 2010. "Immigration and the SPLC: How the Southern Poverty Law Center Invented a Smear, Served La Raza, Manipulated the Press, and Duped Its Donors." *Backgrounder.* http://cis.org/immigration-splc.

Kelley, Angela Maria, and Ann Garcia. 2012. "A Post-Election Look at Immigration Reform." Washington, D.C.: Center for American Progress. http://www.americanprogress.org/issues/immigration/ news/2012/11/09/44676/a-post-election-look-at-immigration-reform/.

Kerwin, Donald. 2002. "Migrants, Borders and National Security: U.S. Immigration Policy Since September 11, 2001." New York: Center for Migration Studies.

———. 2006. "Immigration Reform and the Catholic Church." Washington, D.C.: Migration Policy Institute.

———. 2013. "The Gang of 8 and Accountable Border Enforcement." *Huffington Post,* May 6. http://www.huffingtonpost.com/donald-kerwin/gang-of-eight-immigration-reform_b_3220803.html.

Kieu, Tram. 2013. "Why Immigration is an Asian American Issue." Washington, D.C.: Center for American Progress.

Kim, Seung Min. 2012. "New Gang of Eight on Immigration." *Politico*, December 7.

———. 2013. "Immigration bill: John McCain Says 'Border Surge' Isn't Certain." *Politico,* July 30.

Kotlowitz, Alex. 2007. "Our Town in the Illinois Town of Carpentersville" *New York Times* Magazine, August 5.

Krikorian, Mark. 2004. Not Amnesty But Attrition: The Way to go on Immigration." *National Review,* March 22.

Kung, Cleo J. 2000. "Supporting the Snakeheads: Human Smuggling from China and the 1996 Amendment to the U.S. Statutory Definition of Refugees." *Journal of Criminal Law & Criminology* 90(4): 1271-1316.

Lerner, Gabriel. 2012. "How many people have really been deported under Obama." *Huffington Post,* March 3.

Li, Shan. 2013. "Hawaii Governor Signs Domestic Workers Bill." *Associated Press*, July 1.

Lipton, Eric. 2013. "As War Ends a Rush to Grab Dollars Spent on the Border." *New York Times*, June 6.

Lizza, Ryan. 2013. "Getting to Maybe," *The New Yorker*, June 24.

Lydersen, Kari. 2006. "Ill. Governor to Announce New Benefits for Immigrants." *Washington Post*, December 13.

Mahtesian, Charlie. 2012. "The GOP's Asian Erosion" *Politico*, November 18. http://www.politico.com/blogs/charlie-mahtesian/2012/11/the-gops-asian-erosion-149083.html.

Marinucci, Carla. 2013a. "Silicon Valley Steps Up Role in Immigration Debate." *San Francisco Chronicle*, July 26.

———. 2013b. "Governor Brown signs Bill Requiring Overtime Pay for Domestic Workers." *San Francisco Chronicle,* September 26.

Martin, Philip. 1995. "Proposition 187 in California." *International Migration Review* 29(1): 255-263.

Medrano, Lourdes. 2011. "Arizona justice: Shawna Forde Death Sentence a Rebuke to Border Vigilantes." *Christian Science Monitor,* February 23.

Meissner, Doris, Donald M. Kerwin, Muzaffar Chishti and Claire Bergeron. 2013. *Immigration Enforcement in the United States: The Rise of a Formidable Machinery.* Washington, D.C.: Migration Policy Institute.

Melber, Ari, 2006. "MySpace, My Politics," *The Nation*, May 30. http://www.thenation.com/doc/20060612/melber.

Mitchell, Chip. 2013. "Proposed Visa Could Tie More Foreigners to Abusive Employers." *WBEZ*, May 9.

NILC (National Immigration Law Center). 2001. "INS Issues Rule Expanding its Authority to Detain Noncitizens Without Charge in Response to WTC and Pentagon Attacks." *Immigrants' Rights Update* 15(6).

———. 2012. "State Immigration-Related legislation, Last Year's Key Battles Set the Stage for 2012." Los Angeles, CA: NILC.

———. 2013. "Inclusive Policies Advance Dramatically in the States, Immigrants' Access to Driver's Licenses, Higher Education, Worker's Rights and Community Policing." Los Angeles, CA: NILC.

Nevarez, Griselda. 2013. "Dreamers' Moms Take to Capitol Hill to Advocate for Immigration Reform." *VOXXI,* July 3.

Oda, Yuki. 2012. "Redefining Family: The American Committee on Italian Migration and the Fourth-Preference Campaign."

Ojito, Mirta, 1998. "Once Divisive, Immigration Now a Muted Issue." *New York Times,* November 1.

Orozco, Manuel, and Rebecca Rouse, 2007. "Migrant Hometown Associations and Opportunities for Development: A Global Perspective." Washington, D.C.: Migration Policy Institute.

Parker, Ashley, and Steven Greenhouse. 2013. "Labor and Business Reach Deal on Immigration Issue." *New York Times,* March 30.

Parker, Ashley, and Michael D. Shear. 2013. "Catholic Push to Overhaul Immigration Goes to Pews." *New York Times*, August 21.

Pear, Robert. 1997. "A Move to Restore Benefits to Some Immigrants." *New York Times,* May 4.

Pear, Robert, and Jim Rutenberg. 2007. "Senators in Bipartisan Deal on Immigration Bill." *New York Times,* May 18.

Persell, Caroline Hodges. 1997. "The Interdependence of Social Justice and Civil Society." *Sociological Forum* 12(2): 149-172.

Preston, Julia. 2012. "Young Immigrants Say it's Obama's Time to Act." *New York Times,* November 30.

Preston, Julia, and Fernanda Santos. 2012. "A Record Latino Turnout, Solidly Backing Obama." *New York Times,* November 7.

Rathod, Jayesh M. 2007. "The AFL-CIO-NDLON Agreement – Five Proposals for Advancing the Partnership." *Human Rights Brief* 14 (3): 8-13.

Rayner, Richard. 1996. "What Immigration Crisis." *New York Times,* January 7.

Rose, Ananda. 2012. "Death in the Desert." *New York Times,* June 21.

Rosenblum, Marc. 2011. "US Immigration Policy since 9/11: Understanding the Stalemate over Comprehensive Immigration Reform." Washington, D.C.: Migration Policy Institute.

Rey, John Carlos. 2012. "What's Going on With the Border Patrol?" *Los Angeles Times,* April 20.

Sachs, Lowell. 1996. "Treacherous Waters in Turbulent Times: Navigating the Recent Sea Change in U.S. Immigration Policy and Attitudes." *Social Justice* 23 (3).

Santos, Fernando. 2013. "Shootings by Agents Increase Border Tensions." *New York Times,* June 10.

Schmidt, Eric. 2001. "Bush Aides Weigh Legalizing Status of Mexico," *New York Times,* July 15.

Schneider, William. 1999. "Prop 187 Backlash." *National Journal,* August 7.

Scribner, Todd. 2013. "Immigration as a "Sign of the Times.""

In *"On Strangers No Longer" Perspectives on the Historic U.S.-Mexican Catholic Bishops' Pastoral Letter on Migration.* edited by Todd Scribner and Kevin Appleby. Washington, D.C.: Paulist Press.

Shapira, Harel, 2013. *Waiting for Jose: The Minutemen's Pursuit of America.* Princeton, NJ: Princeton University Press.

Siegel, Loren. 2012. "Communications Research: Talking Immigration Issues: Three Studies." New York, NY: Opportunity Agenda. http://opportunityagenda.org/files/field_file/three_immigration_studies.pdf.

Silva, Mark. 2013. "Immigration Bill: Promise with a Prayer." *bloomberg.com*, May 16. www.blomberg.com/political-capital/.

Singer, Audrey, and Nicole Prchal Svajlenka, 2013. "Immigration Facts: Deferred Action for Childhood Arrivals (DACA)." *Brookings Institute Report.* Washington, D.C.: Brookings Institute.

So, Hemmy. 2006. "Minuteman Project to Launch U.S. Caravan," *Los Angeles Times,* May 3.

Southern Poverty Law Center. 2001. "Anti-Immigration Groups." *Intelligence Report* 101. http://www.splcenter.org/get-informed/intelligence-report/browse-all-issues/2001/spring/blood-on-the-border/anti-immigration-.

Steinhardt, Rachel. 2013. "Promoting Economic Prosperity by Welcoming Immigrants." *Communities and Banking.* https://www.bostonfed.org/commdev/c&b/2013/summer/promoting-economic-prosperity-by-welcoming-immigrants.htm.

Suro, Roberto. 1999. *Strangers Among Us, Latino Lives in a Changing America.* New York, NY: Vintage Books.

Tabirian, Alissa. 2013. "GAO: Current Method of Measuring Border Security is Incomplete." *cnsnews.com*, June 28. http://cnsnews.com/news/article/gao-current-method-measuring-border-security-incomplete.

Tavernise, Sabrina. 2013. "For Medicare, Immigrants Offer Surplus, Study Finds." *New York Times*, May 29.

Teegen, Hildy, Jonathan P. Doh and Sushil Vachani, 2004. "The Importance of Nongovernmental Organizations (NGOs) in Global Governance and Value Creation: An International Business Research Agenda." *Journal of International Business Studies* 35(6): 463-483.

Center for Immigrants' Rights. 2012. "The NSEERS Effect: A Decade of Racial Profiling, Fear, and Secrecy." University Park, PA: Pennsylvania State University Dickinson School of Law. http://www.rightsworkinggroup.org/sites/default/files/RWGPenn_NSEERSReport_060412.pdf.

Tichenor, Daniel. "The Politics of Immigration Reform in the United States, 1981-1990." *Polity* 26 (3): 333-362.

Treaster, Joseph B. 1993. "Immigration Board Rejects Sheik's Plea for Asylum." *New York Times,* July 10.

Tumlin, Karen. 2004. "Suspect First: How Terrorism Policy is Reshaping Immigration Policy." *California Law Review* 92(4): 1173-1239.

Tung, Larry. 2009. "Making New York Immigrant Friendly." *Gotham Gazette,* October 25.

USCIS (U.S. Citizenship and Immigration Services). 2013. "Deferred Action for Childhood Arrivals: September 2013." http://www.uscis.gov/sites/default/files/USCIS/Resources/Reports%20and%20Studies/Immigration%20Forms%20Data/All%20Form%20Types/DACA/daca-13-9-11.pdf.

Vargas, Jose Antonio. 2011. "My Life as an Undocumented Immigrant," *New York Times Magazine,* June 22.

———. 2012. "We Are Americans, Just not Legally" *Time Magazine,* June 25.

Volpp, Leti. 2002. "The Citizen and the Terrorist." UCLA Law Review 49: 1575-1600.

Wang, Ted, and Robert Winn. 2006. "Groundswell Meets Groundwork, Recommendations for Building on Immigrant Mobilizations." Sebastopol, CA: Grantmakers Concerned With Immigrants and Refugees and the Four Freedoms Fund. http://www.mrss.com/news/Groundswell-Report_Final.pdf.

Watanabe, Teresa. 2006. "Mahony's Lenten Message Irritates Some at Service." *Los Angeles Times,* March 2.

Waslin, Michele. 2012. "DHS & NSEERS Program, While Inactive Continues to Discriminate." *Immigration Impact.* Washington, D.C.: American Immigration Council.

Weiner, Tim. 1993. "Pleas for Asylum Inundate System for Immigration." *New York Times,* April 25.

Wilson, Simone. 2011. "John and Ken Broadcast Cellphone Number of LA Immigrant Rights Director, Invite Onslaught of Racist Voice Mails." *LA Weekly Blog.* September 8.

Wong, Carolyn. 2006. *Lobbying for Inclusion, Rights politics and the Making of Immigration Policy.* Palo Alto, CA: Stanford University Press.

Wong, Kent, Janna Shadduck-Hernandez, Fabiola Inzunza, Julie Monroe, Victor Narro, and Abel Valenzuela, Jr. 2012. *Undocumented and Unafraid.* Los Angeles, CA: UCLA Center for Labor Research and Education.